Whistling
in the
Dark

Whistling in the Dark

Personal Essays

LUCIENNE S. BLOCH

BOLD STORY PRESS
WASHINGTON, DC

Bold Story Press, Washington, DC 20016
www.boldstorypress.com

First edition: April 2023

The following essays in this book have
been previously published:

Raritan
"An Island Education" (Winter 2006)
"Sounding the Territory" (Summer 2008)
"Pages from a Daybook" (February 2023)

North American Review
"365 New Words a Year: October" (Summer 2010)

Southwest Review
"The Machine and I" (Spring 2013)

Sewanee Review
"What Is Left" (Fall 2016)

Five Points
"Inside Stories" (Winter 2020)
"Glassworks" (Winter 2021)

Figlit (online)
"The Persistence of Yellow" (May 2022)

Library of Congress Control Number: 2022921447

ISBN: 978-1-954805-44-6 (paperback)
ISBN: 978-1-954805-45-3 (e-book)

Text and cover design by KP Design
Author photo © Emily Kohlberg

Printed in the United States of America
10 9 8 7 6 5 4 3 2 1

To my family, past and present,
whose wise advice and support carried me to this page

Contents

An Island Education

English was my second language, learned in America when I was a young child in the early 1940s. Like many immigrants to any country, I was eager to invest my new language with dazzling magical powers. Speak it, and presto! I would be transformed, an American. Wishes were one thing, reality another. For my refugee family, English was the language of dislocation and difference. It rang with the hearty music of safety, but it didn't feel snug or homey. It was bittersweet in our mouths, unintendedly ironic, flagging the polarity that charged our lives here, the opposites of belonging and otherness, of lucky escape and unspeakable doom. Those pulls felt stronger than any language we spoke, truer than the happenstance of nationality. Accommodating both magnetic fields was a necessity, a challenge, and a recurring dilemma. It was also, I believed, my index of meaning. I saw myself as a walking talking bridge between old world and new, loss and life. A big bridge for a little girl. Even then, I knew it was too big, too slippery.

I tried to accentuate the positive, as the popular song urged. English, homey or not, was a help. I concentrated on absorbing its peppy affable voice, so unlike the mincing hissy dignity that I heard in French, my native language. I liked the generosity of English, with its lavish spread of words to choose from, some plain as boiled potatoes, some fancied up for company, one or another hitting the spot. I parroted the American slang and idioms that I heard on radio programs; if I sounded like a cultural ventriloquist's chatty dummy, fine! Reading the adventures of Tom and Huck, the Bobbsey twins, Paul Bunyan, Nancy Drew, primed me with the fuel of American stories. In pre-television years, magazines and movies provided visual tips about the regional quirks of my new nation and the customs of its far-flung inhabitants. When *Life* went to a demolition derby in Amarillo or a 4-H Club jamboree in Oskaloosa, I was there too. Movies were more thoroughly instructional than photographs in a magazine, more useful, at first, than the secondhand stuff of other lives described in books. Movies showed flesh-and-bone people in action, gave me physical gestures to rehearse and clearly contextualized situations to study, even though it was equally clear that drama and heroics and glamour were rare in everyday experience. Still, anything might happen to anyone. Wasn't that American? The roomy democracy of chance?

Despite all the larky positive noise I made and heard in my new language, despite my lingering wishful thoughts about its transformative magic, speaking English didn't deflect or lighten the dense silences I heard at home, expressive and emphatic omissions. For many years after we arrived in America, my parents balked at talking about the thing that most disturbed their children: the war that sent us here. They must have discussed it together, and with other grownups, but not with us. Too much was left to our raw shaky imaginations. I dreamed of bombs with vultures' razor-sharp beaks, of trains crammed with powdery crumbled chalk, of blue numbers etched on eyeballs, of skin curling and blackening like vegetable peelings in a hot pan, of thick smoke spiraling bright faces into thin air. I forced myself to dream in English. Children died in other languages.

There were other dilemmas in my childhood, less extreme for sure, more like puzzles. Churchill's comment about Russia approximated what the adults in our large close family felt about America, that it was "a riddle wrapped in a mystery inside an enigma." We children could amuse ourselves with silly jokes and riddles if we wished, but our new nation's mysteries and enigmas were daunting, possibly treacherous, prudently put on hold by our family elders for a generation, if not two.

An immediate local puzzle was the city we lived in. New York wasn't America. Everyone said that, not just our expatriated relatives and friends who were grateful for the city's blatant worldliness. Cosmopolitanism was an umbrella; beneath it, Jews could keep their heads dry enough, in America anyhow, presumably. Warsaw, Berlin, Paris, Vienna, Budapest, Amsterdam had all been cosmopolitan cities. When the European skies split, the umbrellas failed to open. That happened there. Here was another story, we hoped. But here wasn't really here. I believed that, although I didn't understand it. How could a city in America not be America? And then one day I heard a remark that had the click of an iconic light bulb in the comic strips I read fervently.

Of New York City's five boroughs, only the Bronx is on the continent of North America; rivers, creeks, channels, and bays separate Manhattan, Brooklyn, Queens, and Staten Island from the mainland. That is a fact. I learned it in 1947. I was in the fourth grade, and we were studying our city. The small progressive school I went to swore by field trips; tests and marks played tenth fiddle to experience, and were seldom given. Learning by doing didn't mesh with my parents' educational principles, nor did the school's permissive milieu reflect their views on proper behavior, but the convenience of a next-door location bested their ideology. In the event, our class took a number of trips over a period of several months. We visited the neighborhood police station, the library on Forty-second Street, Grant's Tomb, the Museum of the City of New York, and City Hall. We didn't meet Mayor O'Dwyer, but we did peek into his office. One morning we took the Broadway subway to Bowling Green, then walked across Battery Park, where we boarded a ferry to the Statue of

Liberty. The water was choppy that gray March day, the harbor seemed vast as an ocean, and perhaps that was what prompted our assistant teacher's statement about the Bronx. It wasn't information we had heard in our classroom, and it wasn't mentioned again. Still, that throwaway remark was a revelation. It clarified an emotional reality that had always perplexed me. In actual topographical fact, my city was mostly detached from the mainland. I lived on the island of Manhattan. It was America, and it wasn't. That was the sort of riddle I appreciated. It was simultaneously direct and devious, like a particular knock-knock joke I enjoyed. Who's there? Orange. Orange who? Orange you glad I said knock-knock? Who's there?

The riddle of my family's resolute insularity seemed largely devious to me, even more convoluted than their regressive insistence on continuing to speak French and other European languages at home long after it was painfully confirmed that they could never return to live in the world they had fled. I thought their arbitrary disengagement from America and its dynamic allure was perverse, unnecessary self-punishment for the noncrime of escaping Europe shortly before the shooting began. I knew what sorrow was. Of sedimentary guilt and remorse, I knew nothing, then.

I worried about inheriting an outsider's perspective. Would I forever see America from an edgy distance? I was old enough by then to know that forever meant only a decade or two. Even so, I felt certain that I would become what I had beheld as a child, as the Whitman poem said I would, verses that our teachers in school admired and declaimed with a purposeful frequency. *There was a child went forth every day, | And the first object he look'd upon, that object he became.* Right, I thought, my future outlook and behavior were already present, sturdily implanted by uprooted parents; self-invention, that most American project, would never be more than an idea for me.

Whitman was only one of the tutelary spirits hovering over the liberal classrooms of the school I attended for twelve lax years. Thoreau, Emerson, John Brown, John Dewey, Freud, Sacco and Vanzetti, Emma Goldman, Samuel Gompers and Eugene Debs, FDR and Eleanor, and the unjustly executed Rosenbergs were among the other mighty presences we felt, some of which conspired to tint our thinking pink, in the euphemism of the era, and contributed to mixing the messages I got. At home, pink was the color of ballet tights or roses in a vase, not a desirable or even acceptable slant of thought. If I had to put a color on my family's political stance, I'd say, yellow. As in scared. The fear was understandable, but nonetheless dismaying. It could happen here, we children were cautioned, a warning substantiated by numerous eyewitness reports of signs on the front lawns of supposedly public American resort hotels: No dogs or Jews allowed. Period. End of grim-faced discussion. Resounding silences, again.

Mixed messages were minor hitches for a child who reflexively felt the push-pull of English. I was so accustomed to ambivalence that it seemed natural to me, almost predictable. There are always two possibilities, as

Jacobowsky wisely said to the foolish Colonel in a play by Franz Werfel, a line that my father liked to quote. Each possibility begat two more that begat two more, to an infinity of outcomes, evidently. My father maintained that Jacobowsky's ballad of two possibilities breathed hope into desperate circumstances. I wondered if a steady breeze of doubt might be more realistic than Jacobowsky's momentary puffs of confidence. That breeze was sorely inadequate, I would discover. Still, skepticism had palpable advantages when mixed messages were sent, by my parents especially. I could usually see both sides of an argument or a quandary, which enabled me to head straight for the middle ground, where I looked for a fence to sit on. A useful strategy at times, a recipe for chicken at others.

I wanted to be brave. I wanted to be happy and funny and popular, a carefree upbeat girl-next-door American. I pretended, with some success, to be some of those things, but I couldn't fool myself. Not when I dreamed those bad dreams, heard the dead howling in the silence of the living, saw a shadowy yawing ghost ship instead of morality's manned vessel displaying its running lights.

In those years when I imagined that speaking English might be my exit visa from fear and foreignness, there were words that had elastic properties for me. "Loophole" was one of them. I knew it meant a narrow opening, and I supposed it might work like the gizmo on the lid of the pressure cooker in our kitchen, a valve that let excess steam escape. Everyone needed to blow off steam occasionally.

Heated quarrels were loopholes. Temper tantrums, back talk, and disobedience were loopholes. I used all those rebellious outlets and then some, constantly picking fights at home because I thought that winning them was a test of my eventual independence from refugees whose nostalgia for their lost irreplaceable world had the slow sure creep of a wasting disease. I believed I was fighting for my life in America, where people set their sights on far horizons, contemplated the big picture, didn't just squint at their own bent figures in a somber stormscape. I was mistaken. Quarreling was an exercise in spit and stress, more of a trap than an out. That legendarily big picture seems smaller now, life-size.

"Particular" was another word with an alternative charge, bouncing from special to fussy. I thought both of those meanings described my extended family: unusual and faultfinding. Still, their detachment from America didn't hinge on jokes about being literally separated from the mainland or on suggestive words. Their insularity went beyond the good fortune of emigrating as a large family group whose members enjoyed each other's company, beyond their conjoint pullback from the unexpected quota systems and restrictions they found here, beyond the gracious domestic theme parks they created to preserve and pass down their European culture. Enhancing those circumstantial consequences, the aftereffects of seeking refuge here, was the insular livelihood they brought with them.

The diamond business was, then, an inherently seclusive and discreet line of work. It operated on the strict rule and proven utility of absolute and reliable confidentiality. People who worked in that business became, or were born, famously secretive. Contracts were never written, a man's word was binding, and deals were sealed with a handshake and a blessing. Disputes weren't settled in the open arenas of civil law courts, but by arbitration before a panel of fellow *diamantaires*, as diamond people called themselves. Profits and losses and inventory were utterly private information, disclosed only to the IRS, and maybe not. The buying, selling, and manufacturing of diamonds is now a heterogeneous global industry, but in my childhood it was, or seemed and sounded so to me, an almost tribal trade, passed from Jewish fathers to sons along with surnames and their dynastic reputations. I naïvely confused the jew in jewelry, making a false lexical link, although it appeared to hold up empirically. Many *diamantaires* belonged to clans that had intermarried for generations, producing a tightly woven web of kinfolk in one zealously hush-hush business. The traditional rites and rituals of the diamond trade didn't change when World War II relocated the commercial center of the industry from Pelikaanstraat in Antwerp to Forty-Seventh Street in Manhattan. The people in the business were changed, for all time, by that war, but the mystique and defects of the closemouthed way they worked was the same as it had been for years on end in another country, in a different universe.

Lurching toward adolescence, I began to do some situational arithmetic. It added up, piece by tenacious piece: the harrowing loaded silences; an instrumental secrecy; the ingrained wobble of outlanders; the historical moment. That limited set of givens included plus and minus factors, pertinent remainders to carry, unwieldy fractions to reduce, real and imaginary numbers, many unknowns. This much was certain: Keeping mum about what mattered was a crucial and complex part of the people who gave me life, love, and their experiential and genetic templates. And transcending any personal models of reticence, far more urgent, was the impact of the recent past. I sensed, just dimly, that silence might be a system of discourse. In that system, at that time, saying nothing was an explicit response to the absence of six million souls. I had no way to check my hunch about that. What I had was an emptiness where there could have been words.

Nature abhors a vacuum, our science/shop/gym teacher declared; our small school had only a few teachers doing several jobs. Cheap, we called that administrative logic. Anyhow, the vacuum. Nature abhors one, I learned, and so, quite soon, did I. Abhor is too harsh. I deplored the emptiness I felt. I wanted to fill it with actual meaningful words, feelings and thoughts expressed aloud, not lurking in the shifty blank spaces between words, between people. Regardless of all that I knew or guessed about my family's secretive natures and occupational conventions, despite all the givens I couldn't choose to return like unwanted mittens or trinkets, I believed there was something wrong, shamefully harmfully wrong, in my parents' reluctance to talk about the horrors that haunted all of us. And I deplored my own cowardly behavior, going along with the hush-up instead of denouncing it. Wasn't it my responsibility, as the firstborn child in our immediate family, to name the monster hiding under our small beds? I had a working voice, didn't I? I had plain strong English, sharp as a knife, to cut through the faulty skin of silence, flense the blubber off, expose the scary troubling vital stuff. How hard would it have been to say, Talk, talk to me! It's here. It's now. It's safe. Speak up, speak out. Tell me the whole terrible story. It's my story too.

I didn't say those simple words. I wouldn't risk getting answers that I might be unable to handle. I felt angry and disappointed with myself when I thought of how much time and emotional energy, mine and my parents', I had spent preparing myself for a part in a drama that, subsequently, I was afraid to stage. All those confrontational scenes and pieces of business, all those daring lines learned by heart, all for nothing. When potential moments of truth about the ghettos, roundups, and death camps arose every once in a while, usually at our dinner table, I didn't seize them. I was silent. I collaborated. I might have shaved my own head, had I known then about that punitive measure.

Of course our lips weren't entirely zipped on the painful subject of the war; it only feels that way now, in prickly recollection of a childhood often informed by unvoiced anguish. My parents did speak about it occasionally, as unalarmingly as they could, their facial expressions a lesson in gravity. And I did ask some questions. After

I turned thirteen, which I took for a critical mass of years, I got up my nerve and asked point-blank about the branches of our family in Poland and Austria. I had more or less correctly anticipated the answer, but when I heard it loud and clear, rocketing out of the abstract and plunging into concrete familial facts, the shock of it was unexpectedly fierce. It was also brief, as deeply jolting episodes can be; the repercussions have lasted a long time. Some of our relatives who perished in the camps were pointed out to me in the few snapshot albums and boxes of photographs that had crossed the Atlantic with us, the others didn't appear in the pictures we had. There were formal studio portraits, outdoor groupings of bearded paunchy men wearing dark suits or long caftans and smiling raven-haired or wigged women in pretty silk dresses with children seated or kneeling on the ground in front of them, some vacation souvenir snaps taken in the mountains or on seaside promenades, occasional pictures of houses, small dogs, shop fronts, a scowling baby in a wicker pram. Names and dates and locations were written under the photos in the albums, but not on the backs of the zigzag-edged paper prints jumbled together in the boxes. For a couple of months, alone in my room at night, with a flashlight under the bedsheets, I pored over the black-and-white and sepia-toned images time and again, as though each new look could reveal more of the terrible story I did and did not want to know, ambivalent as ever. Like a pirate marking a hidden-treasure map, I penciled tiny faint Xs over the heads of family members lost in the camps. They were my connection to the story, theirs were the faces that lived and died it. Then summer came, I was returning to camp in Maine, merely sleep-away, I couldn't help thinking of that difference, though I knew it was a sin to let any such comparison even cross my mind. The more I tried to forget that unforgivable thought, the more worthless I felt, lower than dirt. Making matters worse, shoddy excuse for a person that I was, I looked forward to summer camp, to years of summers in cabins in pine groves, to synchronized swimming, long rainy-day games of follow-my-fancy jacks, to friends from Ohio, canoe tests, swatting pesky no-see-ums, and hiding in the woods behind the rec hall for forbidden smokes. The night before I left for Maine, I put the photo albums and boxes back in our storage closet in the front hall. I did not erase the Xs.

Decades have gone by, and I still don't know the whole terrible story. I know more than I did and, as before, it is not enough, and too much. I would like to think that I outgrew my little yellow slicker of existential dread, but I still can't fool myself about that. Time hasn't sanitized my formative fears and dreams about the destruction I escaped by a near miss. I continue to feel unworthy, of what exactly I don't know. I have stopped wishing on English, as on a star or on birthday candles, to make me a real American; I always knew my wish wouldn't, couldn't, come true. Make-believe American is an option, but less useful than it seemed to my young self in the years when this nation's melting pot myth was alive but fading fast, just about ready to give up the ghost. My children are and feel thoroughly grounded in America, despite having European refugee parents and being bilingual. Their cultural authenticity was never a question, let alone a dilemma. I still feel betwixt and between, accommodating opposite pulls, neither here nor there, not this or that, splitting the difference, a compromise on legs. This is an actual feeling, though not a demonstrable fact. I still see a big bridge as an emblem of my received meaning. I also span the passage of years; there is ample meaning in that, more than I ever envisioned.

What I wonder now is: How indelible are those Xs? What is the generational shelf life of that dark compelling preoccupation I had, still have, with events I didn't experience firsthand, with people I didn't hear when Zyklon B hissed into the inescapable room? Could that preoccupation, more public now, of broader concern and attention, become a permanent fixture in the human mind? Or will it persist chiefly in the collective memory of my ancestral kind? If there are answers to these loose questions, I don't have them. I have language that fails, yet again, to deliver, a thin string of words, spit in the wind, a noise, at least, resonant noise.

Inside Stories

I used to visit an elderly woman who lived in a single room in an apartment hotel on Broadway and 85th Street. Mrs. Palatschinke, so nicknamed because of the crêpes she invariably fed her guests with a glass of tea, was my maternal grandfather's cousin's widow, largely alone in the world, though with a few other distant relatives who pitched in to support her. She also had a clutch of gin rummy, gossip, and strolling companions who congregated in the hotel lobby and dining room. Still, family was family, and alone could be alleviated: two good reasons for the monthly Sunday afternoon visits my mother made to her, often taking me along for reasons that didn't seem so good to me then. Mrs. P and my mother chatted in German, a language I couldn't follow at the gallop they spoke it, so I tuned out their talk, which gave me time to wonder about Mrs. P's room and its puzzling contradictions. Even as I was cramming jam-filled crêpes into my mouth, I could taste the acid of loss in that place, the sharp and drastic difference between full and empty that Hitler had forced on Mrs. Palatschinke's life. Yet despite its meager and lonely reality, Mrs. P's room seemed lively to me, crowded and exciting in ways I couldn't see, hear, or touch. I must have sensed even then that its true contents were intangible. The odd thing is, I can't recall Mrs. P's face. Her hotel room, however, remains crystal clear.

These things were apparent: a narrow bed with a plaid coverlet; a single window looking onto Broadway; a sink in a corner with a mirrored cabinet on the wall above it; a bureau with a brown Philco radio on top of it, flanked by two brass candlesticks; a small table and wooden kitchen chair; a gooseneck lamp next to Mrs. P's Hebrew-Hungarian prayer book on the nightstand; an armchair with a blue slipcover; a picture of New York City in horse-and-carriage days; an electric hotplate and a kettle on a metal cabinet beside the sink. The bathroom was in the public corridor, as was the telephone. Of her pre-war life with its abundance of relatives, friends, and belongings, Mrs. P managed to save only one thing: her own skin. Most fortunately she never had children, she once said to my mother, her speech slowed by a sigh so deep that it caught my attention, and I understood her German and her meaning. Lost people aside, the rest— her home, her possessions, her urbane doings—seemed to be present in that room, but not actually there. I could feel that, believe it, though I couldn't explain it. I was eleven when she died, there wasn't much I could explain.

These days, I can appreciate Mrs. Palatschinke's imaginative feat. She wasn't out of touch with the reality of her situation, but refused to let loss describe or constrict her. Her presence on earth was miraculous, a gift to make the most of. She was clearheaded, aging naturally, not dead before her time like those people she mourned. What I sensed in Mrs. P's little room was the effect of the brave and magical synecdoche she practiced in it, making a part stand for the whole, a gesture for an event, enhancing her now with the fullness of her then. In her characteristic resolve, manner, hospitality, her charm, she made that small room evoke a house on a hill overlooking the Danube in Budapest. One blue chair was an elegant salon, a plateful of palatschinken was a soup-to-nuts dinner party, the Philco a box in the opera house on Andrássy Avenue, one hotel-supplied picture of New York City in horse-and-buggy days was a collection of Jugendstil paintings, one window a terrace with a panoramic view of a beautiful city. Details about Mrs. P's former home and fortunate circumstances were supplied by my mother many years later, when I asked her about the elderly woman we used to visit, whom she had visited several times in Budapest when she was in her teens. Those vivid particulars were the stuff of Mrs. Palatschinke's fictive magic, her sheer pluck and verve that conjured up a complete world out of absences, an easier world to dwell on.

As a graduation-from-college gift, my parents gave me a strictly budgeted two-week trip to Europe. I spent those weeks in Paris, in a bargain-basement hotel on the Rue Bonaparte. This was in the now archaic era when you could squeak by on five dollars a day if you didn't mind the intestinal fanfare trumpeting an unsatisfied appetite; breakfast was included with the room, thankfully. I had never traveled alone before, never stayed more than two or three days in Paris, and never in a so-called student hotel. Still, I figured I might never get another chance to live on my own, even briefly, in that legendary milieu. I figured correctly, as it turned out.

My room was on the sixth floor, at the top of the building; there was no elevator. The moment I first opened its door, I was struck by that room's powerful odor, a compound of tobacco, cheese, and traces of piss. It reminded me of Goethe complaining about the smell of rotten apples that Schiller kept in his desk drawer and sniffed for inspiration, which prompted me to imagine that garret had a story to tell me, "Portrait of the Artist as a Young Nose" was its title, mine on a squatter's spurious claim. Needless to say, I had writerly yearnings. Why else was I was in Paris, on the Left Bank in particular? Because in the days of the giants...

The giants were long gone. The smell in that room was intensely present. The Nose breathed deep, inhaling the perfume of maybes. The lack of light in there was as promising as the furniture: a dogmatic less-is-more statement. There was a bed, a cubby for clothes, a cold-water-only sink, a rickety desk and armless wooden chair, and a grimy dormer window facing an interior light well that didn't do its job. Air wafted in when I opened the window, which I had to do on my knees because the ceiling slanted steeply, but only a hint of daylight entered that room. I considered buying a flashlight or candles to supplement the one low-wattage bulb screwed into a socket on the ceiling, and decided against upping the illumination. I thought of the ambient dimness as a sort of murky bog out of which anything might surface. Anything and everything.

Although I spent many more hours out of that spartan room than in it, loitering in fabled cafés where I rationed myself to bottled water, finding the streets and sights I had read about, soaking up the ethereal elixir of bygone greats, eating a salad in *buvettes* that served, grumblingly, such skimpy meals, it wasn't until after I climbed six flights of stairs and was back in my room that I had a sense of being where I hoped to belong. It was a stirring sensation, as irresistible as gravity. Move over, old-timers, the Young Nose is here. To say that I thought wishfully is to grossly minimize the case. I was a sitting duck for fantasy.

That's what the trouble was: my fuzzy view of that room's real story. I could see that the bleak setting was suitable for a tale about the rigors of writing. I could sample the confining solitariness essential to that line of work. I could envision previous occupants there, characters in the narrative. I could even, and did, shameful to confess, try to push my inclusion in the story by writing a few seriously lame poems in that garret. But I couldn't ram my muddled version of that room down its throat. I didn't stand a chance against its grim eloquence.

Nine days passed before I acknowledged that room's no-nonsense text, and it wasn't what I wanted to know. It told me about failure. The stink of it. The dark of it. Its abrasive and unrelenting discouragements.

I didn't check out of the hotel until the day I flew home, but every waking minute I spent in that attic was a minute of misery. I resented that mean unforgiving room. I felt it had betrayed me, crushed my nerve and dreams with its rigorous matter-of-factness. I didn't like its flinty tone. I was afraid of the failure it described, a stark and daunting probability. I didn't want to consider its guarantee of disappointments. Even so, decades later, recalling the impressionable young hopeful in that room, I have to say that I am glad the Nose wasn't closed to recognizing the harsh underside of a pursuit that it took at face value. I wanted a welcome, and what I got was a warning I needed: Thin ice ahead. And still foreseeable.

My ob-gyn's waiting room looked like a shrine to the divinities of chintz: various flower-patterned fabrics covered the chairs and two sofas, curtained the windows, even the carpet was floral, teeming with full-blown red roses. It was an appropriate look for a room where fertility was conspicuously evident in the bodies of women waiting, waiting, waiting. The doctor routinely ran late in seeing his office patients, never less than two hours, often longer if he had a surgical emergency or had to rush to Mount Sinai's delivery room. We sat there restively, stood to stretch our aching backs, flipped through magazines for the umpteenth time, harassed the receptionist about the vexing delay, lined up to use the payphone, stole out for a quick cigarette on 79th Street, relieved our bladders with a frequency that bordered on absurd, and mostly we talked, ad hoc associates in the business of expecting. My three pregnancies felt like forevers of edgy waiting, especially in that doctor's office, waiting for him to palpate my uterus as a means of checking on the growth of my unborn child, use his stethoscope to listen to its heartbeat, lecture me about weight gain, attempt to allay my natural worries by telling me everything was A-OK, his standard phrase. This was before the availability of helpful information provided by sonograms, amniocentesis, and pre-pregnancy genetic testing.

In that garden-like room I marked time in, the women came and eventually went, talking not of Michelangelo but of this and that, small talk. As a rule, our conversation was deliberately light. We chatted effusively, collegially, about toddler siblings' tantrums of jealousy, stellar and so-so pediatricians, the forgettable pain of labor, the freebie diaper-service photos that routinely distorted the darling faces of our infants, nursery schools, the merits and drawbacks of breastfeeding, playground protocols, and more of the distracting same. We resolutely avoided talking about what mattered most: The suspenseful burden of our ignorance about the unimpaired well-being of the babies curled in our wombs, unborn, unsnuggled, a mystery. Silencing that subject was a group effort, simple enough: We choked it with chit-chat. Why tempt fate by talking about the collective dread in that flowery room's unadorned mystery story? We were wading through it individually, waddling is more like it, page by monthly page of internal clues, suspicions, incidental complications, waiting for the surprise ending to reveal itself, a good or a bad one.

My daughters' ob-gyns' waiting rooms, in which I occasionally sat with them, sited a less iffy story, less veiled, equally engrossing, no less slow to unfold.

The music room was on the second floor of a townhouse in the East Seventies on the island of Manhattan. It was also elsewhere for me, for a while. Notional contexts aside, it was a functioning music room, spacious enough for two pianos, a Steinway and a Bechstein. Framed pages of composers' manuscripts hung on the walls, a row of antique metronomes marched like soldiers along the mantel over the fireplace, piles of scores occupied a bookcase next to the door, six wooden music stands congregated one corner, and twenty or so folding chairs were stacked in another corner, seating for guests at the frequent musicales given by the owner of the house, a doctor who was a gifted amateur pianist. He was my mother's best friend/compatriot/confidant/ opera buddy/medical guru/personal adviser/more? He was my boss one high-school summer when, for lack of another salary-paying opportunity, I subbed for his one employee while she was on a long vacation. His medical office was on the ground floor of the house, in which he lived alone. His wife, a not-so-secret alcoholic, was gone with the wind of divorce; his two adult children had moved to Maine and Oregon. I answered the phone, greeted patients, tidied the bathroom, ran the autoclave, arranged the magazines in neat rows, watered the plants, fetched our lunches from a coffee shop on Lexington Avenue, and hunt-and-peck typed up his scribbled notes and reports to other physicians.

Twenty-four years later, the doctor was my landlord. I was looking for a place to work, and he kindly agreed to let me use his music room on weekdays until 1 p.m., he used it himself after that, playing the piano for hours on end. His practice had dwindled to a handful of people as elderly as he was by then, and he saw patients only in the mornings. I insisted on paying him rent, which I knew he could use. We were both heavy-hearted when, soon after I began working there, he told me he needed to sell the house in the near future.

The music room faced a paved-over backyard with a single tree in it, a scraggly ailanthus. Its leaves shaded the window next to the card table I used as a desk. The summer light in that room was greenish, underwatery. I was in over my head there anyhow, swamped by that room's chimerical suggestions, though not right away. For four months I tried to get going on a novel, rummaged for ideas and characters to animate them, stalked plot lines, made false starts, snatched pages out of my typewriter and balled them up in fits of exasperation. Mostly, I produced a dense fog of angst about not finding anything worth thinking about, sinking my teeth and time into, sorting out on paper.

One drizzly November morning, desperately seeking narrative juice, it occurred to me that there were sounding boards in the room, in the pianos. An idea! Quirky but potential. I grabbed it because it was there and I needed it. Over the next ten days, I outlined a two-part tale for the pianos to tell, a sort of conjugal fugue, a progressively intricate story about the marriage of a musical wizard and his increasingly disenchanted wife. The Bechstein, with its softer sound, would speak for the woman. Whose lives would I mine for my fictional characters? Wolfgang and Constanze? Hector and Harriet? Gustav and Alma? I chose the Mahlers. After all, the doctor whose house I was in and my mother came from Vienna. I knew a little something about life in that city, its hangover of imperial grandiosity, its café, musical, and *Küss die Hand* cultures, its gusto for melodramatic scandals, its facile seductiveness.

I made a big mistake that rainy morning many years ago. Those ivory keys opened an empty box. It took me eight months and one-hundred-and-twenty-two pages to see, in a flash of frank appraisal, that there was nothing in it, nothing but stale hot air. I was furious with myself for not seeing that sooner, for opportunistically snatching a lousy suggestion, for faking every character, place, word of dialogue, and episode on those pages, for wasting my time on a long-haul flight to nowhere. I squared the stack of pages, divided it into tearable parts, and reduced those pages to shreds. I dumped the scraps into the fireplace, lit a match, and began to burn them. I heard the doctor rushing up the stairs and into the room. "I smell fire!" he shouted. It's me raging, I didn't say. I apologized for alarming him, and quickly smothered the fire with the bucket of sand on the hearth.

That's when he told me the house was sold, I had to leave by the end of the next month. It was good news to me, after that galling hour of truth. I was so relieved to hear it that I packed up and decamped the next day. It was the only move I made there that was not a mistake. If there's an Aesopian moral to the gimmicky fable I inflicted on that room and myself, it might be: The music is not for rent.

I use the kitchen in our apartment several times a day, and every now and again my mind's ear wanders, listens to the history of women in that room, in most kitchens. The herstory, I should say in PC-speak, a language so picky and pushy that I hesitate to use it for fear of garbling its newly-minted jargon. Okay, so I am chronologically challenged, and so damn what. I am also chronologically charged, and not with nostalgia.

I might not hear echoes of the past in my kitchen if it were definitively contemporary. But it isn't, and I do. That high-ceilinged room looks and substantially is the same as the first day it was used. The paneled wooden cabinets, drawers, broom closet, pantry cupboards are original, installed when the building's construction was completed in 1921. I sometimes wonder about the women who worked in my kitchen before me. Was the first one a triumphant suffragette? Was there a snazzy flapper stuffing naked Thanksgiving turkeys in there? The mother of a marine who died on Guadalcanal?

I did meet, just once, the woman who lived in the apartment before we moved into it. She changed bits and pieces of the kitchen over the decades she used it and, except for a paint job and major appliances, we lived with her decorative alterations. The floor was forties patterned linoleum, the counters were orange Formica that shrieked Rise and Shine! to the fifties, the overhead fluorescent tubing was popular in the sixties, as were the curved-front metal cabinets with push-button latches below the rounded counters near the kitchen and pantry sinks. After years of talking about it, we finally did a minimal renovation. The floor was replaced by vinyl tiles that simulate terracotta, track lighting was installed, the sticky drawers were planed and retrofitted with metal glides, the counters were rebuilt and are now white, still Formica, with a course of Mexican tiles above them.

That is all we changed in our kitchen, and it feels to me like newish wine in an old bottle, not appreciably different or updated. I make our customary meals in there, my husband and I ordinarily eat in there, our grandchildren drop mac-and-cheese glop on the floor, we age in a bottle that was corked long ago. Inevitably and naturally, there will be sediment in a wine bottle. My kitchen's sediment is the residual presence of women in it, the recurring sounds and silences of their passage through time, in their traditional place.

I stand at the sink washing lettuce, scramble eggs, make soup, slice bread, clean countertops, empty the dishwasher, iron pillowcases, do what needs doing, and I sense generations of women keeping me company in my kitchen, in home kitchens anywhere: wives, daughters, mothers, sisters, friends, grandmothers, household help, aunts, in-laws, some strong, some weak, the glad and the regretful, the angry and the forbearing, the lost and found souls, women who spent years and years in kitchens instead of designing bridges or performing brain surgery or heading multinational think tanks. It may be that some of the women who lived in our apartment before us had professions or jobs outside of the house, taught or took classes, were active in civic, philanthropic, political, and cultural organizations, traveled widely, but what I hear in my head in my kitchen are women's everyday domestic noises and same old stories: the constant meals, chores, messes, the routine tedium, seemly housewifery, the self-disappointments, stories amplified by the clatter of chopping, pounding, shaking, beating, cracking. I know those old stories have lost some traction these days, but they come with my kitchen's outmoded territory, with my own, and continue to weigh on me, pull at me. I don't have the option of selective amnesia, wouldn't use it if I did, wouldn't devalue the work of women in kitchens by forgetting about its timeless commonality and importance. So I keep hearing those echoes, imagined perhaps but true-life stories, too real, even now, too prevalent, too resonant to dismiss.

The Machine and I

The other day I saw a reference to a remark made by Jack Warner, of Hollywood moguldom in the glory years of movie studios. He called writers "schmucks with Underwoods." This quip could be incomprehensible to most people under the age of forty, computer users who may never have seen a typewriter, let alone know its brand name, but for me it is a fully-loaded comment.

At my father's well-intentioned insistence, I took a six-week typing course during the summer before I started college in 1955; the progressive school I went to would have sooner closed its high-minded doors than offer such utilitarian training to its students. My father's reasoning was, typing skills would come in handy over the next four years and, even more farsightedly, I could always get a respectable job in a nice office if by some misfortune

I failed to find a husband during those years or subsequently. He was a naturally pragmatic thinker. He was also attuned to the mentality of that conventional era. So was I, like it or not.

Mondays through Fridays, I took a crosstown bus twice a day, joining the crowd of regular office workers. From 9:30 a.m. to 4:30 p.m. with an hour off for lunch, I sat at a desk on the ground floor of a brownstone on 75th Street between Madison and Park Avenues. This so-called garden apartment housed the Claire Lux Secretarial School. My father did some research before I was sent there. The popular Katherine Gibbs school did not offer a short-term course, and the conveniently uptown smaller Lux school was, he assured me, "an outfit of the first water." I got his gist, though I could have used a gloss on "first water." The outfit was good enough to last over the decades with its name and stated purpose unchanged, unlike newer generations of women whose aims and opportunities are broader. I suppose the school trains all genders of office personnel these days, computer keyboards made competent typing a polymorphic plus. It is currently located on Third Avenue, according to the Manhattan phone book that I consulted yesterday out of idle curiosity. I don't intend to call or visit the place or its website, if it has one. I don't want its now to impinge on my then.

Smaller indeed. There were three students the summer I learned to touch-type, five unoccupied desks, one instructor, Miss Lux herself; she taught a course in shorthand, but no one had signed up for it during those six weeks. Miss Lux had probably crossed the Great Divide of sixty, so she can't have lasted as her eponymous school has, but she was somewhat girlish: a bit sappy, impatient, flippant, demonstrably moody. Even so, she had a schoolmarm's platitudinously strict edge, though she didn't use a ruler on our wayward hands, her sharp tongue did the job. She dressed young, in white linen blouses, often with cutwork decoration, and mid-calf floral-print or faux-peasant cotton skirts above black Pappagallo flats. This resembled what her students, actual girls, wore in the heat of summer, but our blouses were sleeveless, our skirts blatantly skimpier, and our waists were accentuated with cinch belts. Shorts and tank tops were not common-place on city streets in those days, and air conditioning was hardly ubiquitous, so we all, Miss Lux included, oozed sweat in that basement with its uncurtained south-facing windows and French doors that led to a treeless brick-paved patio. The sweat trickled down our arms and dripped onto the keys from the palms of our hands that were poised over them just so, eyes fixed forward or sideways or sometimes closed, in line with Miss Lux's directive of the moment. When our fingers skidded uncontrollably across the puddled keys we were allowed to stop typing and wipe our hands and brows and keyboards with our soon-soggy cloth hankies. Fortunately, there were only two serious heat waves during the six weeks of the course. The lavender-tiled pharmacy on that corner of Madison Avenue had a soda fountain where I ate lunch every day, alone because the other girls lived nearby and went home to eat. The place was cooled by ceiling fans, and I dawdled unconscionably over my chicken salad sandwiches to benefit from the breeze. That pharmacy has also lasted, in a much larger more deluxe incarnation across the avenue, and though it no longer has a lunch counter I sometimes smell the ghost of bacon past in there, a tangy notional undernote to the cloying perfumes in the air.

The course began with the continual typing of "the quick brown fox jumps over the lazy dog" and other phrases that use the whole alphabet. I had endured years of ineptitude at piano keyboards, but a typewriter's keyboard looked and felt manageable from day one, and not only due to my having mastered the ABC's in kindergarten. Perhaps it was the suggestive effect of what Miss Lux called the "home" keys on the machine's middle row of alphabetic keys, or the predictable response of pressure on a specific key, or the lightly dimpled surface of all the keys that welcomed the fleshy pads of fingertips. For all or any or none of those reasons, I got the hang of the QWERTY scheme of things to Miss Lux's satisfaction a few days before the other girls did.

Then, nearly two full weeks into the course, we turned our eyes to sample letters and texts placed to the left of our office-size Smith Corona manual typewriters. Miss Lux used a kitchen timer to clock our half-hour shifts of typing. "Count those words, young ladies, mark your errors, subtract three from the total for every mistake, and divide by thirty," she invariably said when we got a short break. I don't know if minus-three-per-error was usual in typing schools or merely Miss Lux's method of calculating proficiency. The proper forms of address and the spacing of business correspondence was an essential lesson, and she gave it six or seven times. We also practiced reversing and changing typewriter ribbons, a messy affair, making carbon copies on onionskin paper, using a narrow strip of powdery white correction tape on our mistakes or, better, a typewriter eraser, a nifty little rubber wheel that sported a bristle-brush goatee on its metal frame. The long and short of it is, I learned to touch-type approximately thirty-eight words a minute, not a great speed, but fast enough to get a dated, hand-signed certificate from the Claire Lux Secretarial School with my name, misspelled, typed in capital letters across the center of it.

I was not sorry when that course ended. I had done what I set out to do. As a reward for not being a lazy dog, my parents gave me a Royal portable typewriter to take to college, a battleship gray metal machine in a taupe brown-flecked hard plastic carrying case. I would have preferred a snazzy red Olivetti or a slim refined Hermes, but the squat plain Royal was what I got.

I didn't uncase my typewriter until the start of my sophomore year, when our class dean suggested, but did not decree, that we hand in typed double-spaced papers to make life easier for our professors. By the time I finished typing three papers, I felt entirely comfortable with my previously untouched Royal. I never told my father that I didn't immediately use my newly certified skills. Besides, he was right about the future of those skills. I graduated

unmarried, unengaged, not pinned or steadily dating
someone, and within a month I was employed as a secretary in a tiny publishing house in Greenwich Village,
although my job title, editorial assistant, grossly misrep-
resented the work, which consisted of taking dictation
and typing. I hadn't learned shorthand, but any college
girl of the 1950s who ever took an art history course
and was able to synchronize looking at slides, smoking, knitting argyle socks, listening to and absorbing an
informative lecture, taking notes, chewing gum, raising
her hand to ask and answer questions, whispering to her
neighbor, fixing her hair, all routinely done in a darkened
classroom, would not need Gregg or Pitman systems of
symbolic writing for an office job.

I typed reams of short or long-winded letters from
the publisher and the editor-in-chief to their literary, ski,
legal, academic, medical, squash, and political buddies,
members of a mutual admiration society that didn't stop
congratulating its collective self for having supported and
accomplished something I definitely did not support: the
release of Ezra Pound from St. Elizabeths Hospital. At
least it wasn't my name at the bottom of those letters, and
I justified my scutwork by frequently reminding myself
that the object of their attention had a proven connection to my college major in English literature. Anyhow,
Pound's freedom was a *fait accom*fucking*pli*.

I used an office-model manual Remington in that
workplace, the management wouldn't spring for an electric typewriter for as lowly an employee as I was. Ditto at
my second job, also in a publishing house, where I had the

same Remington, but a newer one, on which I typed generally negative reports from notes hastily scribbled by the overworked slush-pile reader whose permanently bleary eyes might have interfered with her critical acuity. An editor would glance at those reports, then tell me to pack up and return the manuscripts with preprinted impersonal unsigned rejection letters. A thankless job. My Royal was locked in its case, parked on the floor of my closet. I lived with my parents and younger sibs, a fairly standard arrangement at the time for single young women who hadn't relocated far away from their family homes.

I met my husband-to-be-and-still-is. We married and set up house. My typewriter and I moved across Central Park, and it went straight into a storage closet. Soon, I would also be in a condition of confinement, as giving birth used to be called. I stopped working two weeks before our first child arrived, on our first anniversary. I didn't go back to an office job, mothering was the full-time work I chose to do. I would have chosen it even if I hadn't been, again, attuned to the era. My Royal aged silently, unseen, unmissed. Any correspondence I had—personal letters, bills, thank-you notes, condolence letters, and invitation cards—was handwritten, another standard practice then, although my scrawl exploded the norms of penmanship as taught in traditional grade schools, but not in the progressive one I attended where halls and classrooms resounded with the din of students stepping, trudging, skipping, stomping, ambling to the music of

their "different drummer," as Thoreau put it in a quote
stenciled on a wall in the school's library.

A second child, a bigger apartment, a third child, and
twelve years later, I began to use a typewriter again, every
weekday morning and early afternoon when nothing
more important arose, which is to say, the light over my
desk was more particle than wave. Still, the pages slowly
added up to a stack of manila file folders filled with short
stories and chapters of two novels, all typed on my old
Royal with its solidly familiar feel and quirks and flaws
and lively companionable clatter.

In the mid-1980s, unable to resist the temptation of
a machine connected to a printer that would spare me
the laborious retyping of draft after draft of work in
habitually snail-paced progress, I decided to switch to a
computer. In the event I might not like using a computer,
and because typewriter supplies and repair shops were
beginning their sure and irreversible slide into disuse, I
had my Royal completely reconditioned, and bought sev-
enty-five ribbons for it, which bought me some time with
it. Xerox copiers had eliminated the use of carbons and
onionskin paper, and liquid Wite-Out replaced correction
tape and the jauntily bearded eraser, so I didn't have to
squirrel away those items.

The first computer I used was called a "luggable." It
seemed less formidable than the hulking multiunit
desktop machines I saw in stores that sold electronic
equipment. Luggables were valise-like boxes you could

open as needed. The keyboard side of the box lay flat on a desk, the computer's controlling brain, guts, fan, and monitor were packed into the other side of the valise that stood upright on the desk: ancestral laptops. Closed, it resembled the encased portable Singer sewing machine my mother used occasionally, a seamstress analogy I didn't truly appreciate then. My NEC luggable had a DOS operating system that ran the bone-simple word-processing program I bought. Text was displayed in flickery green letters on a gray screen. Document files were saved internally on the C-drive, and safe extra backup was done on 3.5-inch hard diskettes inserted into the A-drive slot on the machine's left side. These diskettes were still called floppies, a nod to the 8-inch flexible copy disks from which they had recently evolved.

I learned to use a computer without a Miss Lux to teach me. After all, its keyboard wasn't a novelty for me, and neither was learning by doing. The machine and the program came with printed manuals, mostly too technical for me to digest. Even so, it was encouraging to browse through the manuals and discover that some of the machine's operational vocabulary echoes the cognitive workings of people using it, not unlike the word "typewriter," which formerly defined both the mechanical device and its human (predominantly female) operator. A computer and I contain storage and retrieval systems, do goal-directed searches, flip-flops, undergo glitches and crashes, and automatically process data in other ways that are categorically baffling to me. Similarities to the machine apart, and beyond the manuals, I needed an instructive method. The one I followed was trial and numerous errors, which led to a near-book-length blunder of prose stricken by rapid jumpy cutting and pasting for no good reason, and which I repeatedly printed on what looked like enough paper to deforest a Catskill mountain. Not to mention the paper wasted on the sides of the roll my dot-matrix printer used, miles of perforated edges I tore off and promptly trashed. The touted promise of paperless offices was and remains a daydream for me.

Eventually, I took charge of the machine and the program instead of letting their facile high-speed functions run me. This happened when I began to see the substantiality of shimmering words that floated, wraithlike, on and off the screen, to sense their pulse, hush, pace, heat, punch, lift, stutter, slump, and other physical qualities that my hands often felt when typing on my Royal with its pinging bell and rhythmical thunks and capricious jiggles and tics and squeaks and direct immediacy of print on paper.

The time came to replace my luggable. Not wanting to put it out with the garbage because it had my notes, narratives, failures, impulsive rants in letters I never printed and mailed, and some personal information stored deep inside it, and not knowing how exactly to purge its C-drive because those pages in the manual were gibberish to me, my husband and I came up with an unusual strategy. We beat that machine to death with a hammer, in the service hall adjacent to our apartment's back door. We covered it with an old sheet to keep the glass and metal shards from flying through the air. It was an oddly gratifying event, two responsible adults behaving like juvenile delinquents gleefully vandalizing a helpful appliance.

I installed my outmoded word-processing program on my new IBM desktop, and kept on accumulating floppies. I also bought an ink-jet printer that used sheets, not rolls, of paper. I learned to empty a C-drive by reading a *Dummies* book, a then-new and still ongoing series of illustrated how-to books for rookies and dabblers in various fields, comparable to a Classic Comics version of *Finnegans Wake*. Two ever-faster computers later, I yielded to a Windows Word program that looks to me like DOS in fussy drag, but can produce and send document files that newer-model computers can read. I keyboard most commands, handle the mouse as seldom as possible. I managed to locate and buy the last machine made with an internal floppy port next to its USB ports, a Lenovo I am nursing though it is already an antique. Had I known that production of the typing paper I favored would soon be discontinued, I would have warehoused a sizable number of those red boxes with a drawing of the Great Sphinx at Giza on their covers, an image hinting at mysteries and riddles to consider and possibly understand on the paper inside of them. At present, I can find dusty boxes of high-density formatted diskettes, ten in each box. I have an ample supply of diskettes. They too will soon be extinct, the trilobites of the Paleotech.

I cling to using floppies as I was and am fondly attached to my retired Royal, jilted is more like it. For artifactual evidence of continuity, I guess, for lost simplicity and tangible particularity, for the click of a diskette fitting into and emerging from its slot, for ballast in a world of ether connectivity, of cloud communication and storage, satellite spycams, distance learning, and so much more of the bit-based like. Every so often, I do additional backups of my work on a flash stick. I know there will only be USB ports, or their newer equivalents, in my very near future.

In the meanwhile, the filled floppies pile up, my Royal sleeps soundly, its ribbons dry out, my fingers are stiff and starting to gnarl, and I still touch-type, hands above the unchanged arrangement of home keys, eyes on the bright screen that waits, cursor blinking impatiently, almost insolently, for the now-lazier schmuck to get moving. Not that anyone is counting, but I don't type thirty-eight words a minute, thirty-eight an hour is speedy for me these days, if I'm lucky. If not, time passes anyway, wordless, unpunctuated, irretrievable, and that's how it goes.

What Is Left

I lost some weight last month. I removed half of the keys I carried for all of my adult life from my key ring, and returned them to the real-estate company whose properties include the apartment that my family rented for seventy-six years. I used those keys constantly after I married, visiting my parents and younger siblings, then my widowed mother, then my brother, who lived there for the past eleven years and died two months ago. The apartment had to be vacated in a couple of weeks, its contents sorted, distributed, sold, donated, stored, or abandoned as junk. Seeing the cartons and large black trash bags pile up, it struck me that death might be the ultimate repo man. After the place was more or less empty, I gave the keys to the landlord.

When I unlock the door to the apartment I live in with my husband, my now-lighter key ring cues a sense of diminishment.

Growing up on the West Side of Manhattan, I rode the 86th Street crosstown bus, officially the M86, several times a week, if not every day. As a college graduate living with my parents, I took the M86 to and from work. When I married and moved to the East Side, I crossed town frequently, soon with young children in tow. In later years, visiting whoever was living, lonely, ailing, needy, dementing, or dying in the apartment on Central Park West, I backed and forthed so regularly I could have approximated a tide chart.

Walking west on 86th Street toward Madison Avenue last week, I saw the M86 at its usual stop on the corner. I began to run towards it when, abruptly, I remembered that I didn't need to take it. I looked at the people getting on, and I ached, actually felt a cramp in my right hand, the hand that is habitually in my purse groping for my Metrocard just before I board a bus. I wondered: Can a missing bus ride feel like phantom limb pain?

It wasn't the ride I missed, it was the people and home I routinely shuttled to see and to be in. Now I need errands, appointments, events, as reasons to take the M86.

Another habit rattles me at present. For more decades than I care to specify, I have taken an early morning walk partway or all around the Reservoir in Central Park. The first thing I invariably notice when I step onto the cinder track is the apartment building where I used to live. Even without looking at it closely, I know its shape and posi- tion on the avenue's line up of architecturally distinct structures, the pale ocher of its bricks, the setbacks of its upper-floor terraces, the spacing of its casement windows facing the park. Now, when I see the windows of my old bedroom, I can't help thinking that the girl I was is still there, in the dust motes on the furniture and fixtures in that room, inside the desk and dresser drawers, floating in the air throughout that apartment. That presence will be dispelled when the apartment is gut-renovated, as the landlord plans. She, I, we're not ready to be torn apart or swept away; we are still useful, still visible in sunlight.

Nor am I ready to forgo a walk or to change my routine, despite what it prompts me to recall, fleetingly most days, at length sometimes, what happened to land us in that apartment: my family's escape from Hitler's Europe.

I would certainly prefer to look straight ahead, even with blinkers on like a skittish horse, but my genes, imprinting, temperament, residential location, and various other recurring or random circumstances and relationships— life, in short—periodically gang up to turn my gaze backward. Besides, preference isn't always a deciding vote I can cast or a plan I can make and stick to. My mind, like everyone's, has some tenacious plans of its own.

Today, for instance, I started counting losses: keys to a home, its former and final occupants, die-hard crosstown habits, the old furniture and particles of my younger self in a room with a view of the Reservoir. I wanted to continue with a sort of love story about my long and lastingly passionate relationship with that captivating body of water, the moods we frequently share in sync—whether placid, icy, befogged, stormy, flat, gloomy, dreamy, troubled, shiny—the enduring proximity of our different beings, our mutual out-of-dateness, the illusory mists we produce. But where am I headed now? Back to the shadows, again. I should have seen this coming.

I could digress, stall out, shilly-shally as usual, run unnecessary errands, take a few days off, repaint the chairs in my kitchen, but those are temporary evasions. Sooner than later, I am in the thick of memories I don't choose to jog, can't ignore or make light of, have to account for and flesh out occasionally, need to dwell on now, and don't want to forget.

A long time ago in Transylvania there were merchants known as shadow traders, briefly mentioned by Frazer in *The Golden Bough*, which I borrowed from the library in college and haven't read again. I don't remember much about that book beyond its title, the author's last name, the fact of its scholarly significance, and the gist of a paragraph or two about shadow traders.

The merchants sold their goods to builders who needed human shadows to enclose in the foundations of the houses they were constructing, a practice that ensured the structure would be sturdy and, importantly, would protect the inhabitants of the house from intrusive enemies. This was in the days when immuring a living person or a corpse was no longer acceptable, and people's shadows substituted for souls that, traditionally, had the powers of guardian spirits. How the traders obtained their merchandise is unclear; it may have involved measuring the length of shadows that sick people cast on the ground before death canceled that opportunity. The cost of those measured shadows and how they were used in the construction process is also obscure. Even so, inexplicable or entirely apocryphal, that legend about the placement and purpose of shadows stayed with me, and surfaces from time to time.

Not so long ago, relatively speaking, I used to gulp down a spoonful of cod liver oil every morning. Although it made me gag, I swallowed that nasty slimy stuff because I wanted to be strong. In addition, I insisted on having Wheaties for breakfast. I wasn't taking any chances. Between the fish oil and the food of champions, I hoped to develop the muscles and guts I needed to crush, or at least repel, the goose-stepping demons who invaded my night-mares. As hopes go, that one was a losing proposition; the other side won. They hadn't won the war, but they beat me and my childish ploys. Still, I didn't give up hoping, not for another few years. Surrender was for quitters.

A schoolmate gave me a diary for my twelfth birth-day, a little blue leatherette book with a shiny brass lock opened by a tiny key. The card with it read: *For your deep dark secrets*. I promptly tossed it in the garbage can out-side the back door of our apartment. I was bursting with secrets, but writing in a diary was too risky. By then I knew what had happened to a girl who kept a diary while she was hidden in an attic in Amsterdam, not far from Antwerp where I was born. There was an ocean between me and what happened to her, but who knew, evil had its own borderless map, its own brutal afterlife.

We did a unit on religions in our ninth grade world history course. Some of the Egyptian deities we studied had animal heads on human bodies. Jackal-headed Anubis, the god of tombs, weigher of dead people's hearts, caught my attention. What was the weight of six million hearts? I was taking algebra that year, but I couldn't find or even estimate that huge unknown factor. What did it reduce to in individual terms? What was the gravitational force of a vast mass of lost people?

There was a lot to figure out as best I could, which wasn't very well. Like many teenagers, I wanted answers, fast, never mind whether they were right, partly right, or dubious. Muddled and uninformed as my adolescent ruminating was, I believed it was definitely sounder than nightmarish wrestling with vicious fiends.

In college I cleared the decks for a steadier course ahead. I deliberately neglected to think about the questions that troubled my girlhood; that disregard was feasible, even advisable, on a campus where many students didn't know Dachau from dachshunds and cared less. There were those who knew and cared deeply but kept it to themselves. This was in the days when people were too anguished or unwilling to publicly bare their raw pain about the horrors of World War II. In the privacy of Jewish family homes, there was occasional mention of roundups, selections, and showers, whispers usually, muffled inside information punctuated by omissive ellipses, hesitational dashes, and full stops of wordless despair. Eventually, that crucial subject was aired loud and clear, but until that happened, mum was the word. Hold your tongue. Forget the past. Look to the future. I heard those snappy cultural commands, and chose to comply.

Maybe it wasn't a choice, it could have been an involuntary reaction. After all, I belong to a generation that was saddled with several labels, some unfairly attached. "Silent" and "apathetic" are among the tags we wore, not surprisingly, considering that we were impressionable children in the years when one often-repeated cautionary slogan was soon supplanted and intensified by another we also heard and heeded: Loose Lips Sink Ships; Duck and Cover.

We did not run, screaming, protesting, from or for anything. We quietly, routinely, crouched below a schoolroom desk or table and hid our heads under our arms when a civil defense siren sounded, responding to the blare like Pavlov's hapless dog. It was a lesson in futility, implausible protection in the event of an atomic attack, in the event of personal threats. But that was what we were trained to do. Some of us overcame our youthful conditioning, and some of us did not. Safety, our formative watchword, was more apt than apathy; we were not silent so much as scared. Outspokenness, political and social activism, defiant counterculturalism, sexual free-and-easiness jump-started by the pill, Stonewall Riots, and *Roe v.*

Wade characterize the generation that came of age in the 1960s and early 1970s, not my era.

Whichever my reaction was, optional or reflexive, the outcome was identical. I shut up, ignored my fears about savage destruction, looked forward to finding what I longed for: some genuine and lasting equanimity.

After graduation from college, I had a job that paid next to nothing. This was a business-world economy based on the insulting but proven premise that young women would ungrumblingly work for cut-rate salaries while waiting for husbands to materialize. Within two years, mine did. I met a man who, like me, was a refugee from Hitler's Europe, though I was an infant when my family emigrated and he was older. If I was inwardly primed for a person who had ground-truthed the map of evil I had only imagined, I was wholly unaware of it. The explicit attraction was love, heady and sure and reciprocal.

My husband's war was as real as the concrete bunkers of the Maginot Line in his native country, his escape as narrow as the cracks I saw on their surfaces some years later. His own story ends well, but there is irreparable damage and tragedy in it, a grandmother, aunt, uncle, and cousins murdered in the camps. There is also an edge of adventure in it, of the chase, of daring. An eleven-year-old boy sticks his head out of a car window, intent on correctly identifying the markings on all the low-flying German planes strafing the roads leading south in France, roads jammed with crowds of people fleeing the Nazis on foot, on bicycles and motor scooters, in cars, vans, prams, wheelbarrows, horse-drawn carts, farm and military vehicles. He tosses sleeplessly in barns and cellars, adding up the amounts his father spends on bribing *fonctionnaires* to get documents that should have been handed over for free. He worries about the money running out before it buys salvation. He crosses mountain borders in the darkness of night, travels to America through seas already bristling with German submarines and minelayers. The long and short of it is, he lived.

The authenticity of his experience put my vicarious fears to shame. I was glad to shove my bogus unearned emotions into a deeper hole than mere neglect could provide, a dank windowless dungeon where I hoped they would waste away, unseen, unheard, forgotten.

In what seemed like lightning speed, I was snugly located in a thriving microcosm, so satisfying that Betty Friedan's unmasking of "the problem that has no name" in 1963 didn't signal even a bumps-ahead stretch on my motherly freeway. I had three babies in six years, and it felt as though procreation's bodily force had necessarily annexed some energy from my mind, which felt natural. What I mainly expressed in those years was breast milk. I was enchanted by my children, and with my purposeful new identity as a parent. O the wonder of it all! The toothless grins, blubbery thighs, winsome first steps and words, even the tears and tantrums were beguiling. It was a paradise of innocence waiting to be lost, in time and inevitably. Meanwhile, it was an abundantly sunny spot.

Out there, beyond my small wonderland, was the larger sphere of change: Vietnam; the Berlin Wall; the assassinations of the Kennedys and King; nuclear test ban, civil rights, and anti-war demonstrations; the Prague Spring; student uprisings; riots in Watts, Detroit, and Newark; men on the moon; Kent State; the Pentagon Papers; women's rights rallies; the Munich massacre; Watergate; the hostage crisis, and other momentous upheavals that shifted at least some entrenched outlooks and doings. I saw the bigger picture constantly in newspapers and on television, examined it in conversation, but it didn't regularly preoccupy my thoughts or alter my activities. I can't produce alibis now for my nonparticipation in marches and rallies, except to point a finger at those old generational constraints, reinforced over the years by my personal ones. I could say: Yes, yes it's reprehensible, sorry I skipped the zeitgeist's road test, but I was busy. This is true, though it can't be certified.

There was a seeming infinitude of Dr. Seuss rhymes, minor illnesses, sandbox melees, Crayola scrawls on walls, bloody knees and noses, playdates that turned on a dime from fun to fights, and chewing gum parked in curly hair. Soon, simple Q&A sessions became heated arguments with teenagers whose hormonal blitzes turned our dining room into a designated hard hat area. I spent nights wide awake wondering if parental speeches about the perils of unprotected sex and hard drugs had any traction at all. In addition, I had wifely, daughterly, sisterly, domestic, sociable, volunteer, and civic occupations: My plate was overfull. It is also true that, when I had a minute for introspection, I glimpsed my idleness from the neck up. My loitering dismayed me, but I assured myself it was temporary, a mutable state of mind, of matter, like a hailstone or a blazing log, only passingly dense. In the near future, I would emerge from the primordial soup of daily mothering, evolve into a different order of being with another existential drive. I wasn't impatient. There was plenty to do, more and more as the years rocketed by with their payloads of busyness.

The inevitable occurred: My Arcadian phase became a museum piece, prized and evocative but not pertinent or adaptable, not sparking more than fond thoughts of times that looked shinier in recollection than at the bleary frazzled moment. After the last of my children fledged, I felt as lost as their innocence. Off they went, one by one, in pursuit of independence, equipped with decisional radar that had some blind spots and false echoes on its screens. One had difficulties for a few years, the other two found their way with comparative ease. Finding mine was not easy or quick, more of a chance event than a sure thing.

For almost three years I looked for work, had fifteen interviews for jobs I didn't get, applied to two graduate schools that didn't admit me, and the less said about my slog through that Sahara of rebuffs, the better.

Then, out of the blue on a blustery January morning,
a job appeared. I was taking my daily half-stride, half-
stroll around the Reservoir when I heard a pounding
noise. I stopped and turned. There wasn't a jogger on
the track behind me. The wind was gusting hard. Was I
hearing nature's din? I happened to glance at the building I grew up in across the white-capped water, saw
the windows of my former bedroom glaring with sharp
yellow light, and I sensed what the pounding was: the
clamor of feelings I had banished to a dungeon many
years earlier. Why those emotions returned on that particular morning still puzzles me. I had looked at that
building, those windows, hundreds of times from one
spot or another on the track circling the water, and never
seen anything but a familiar shape in the panorama of
the skyline, never pictured light-struck windowpanes
as reproachful eyes, never heard strange sounds. I can't
verify the surreal experience I had that cold windy Tuesday many years ago, I can only vouch for its effect on
me. The troubling feelings I had hoped to forget didn't
wither and die. They were back, unexpectedly present
and fierce as ever, banging on the walls I had built to
confine them, demanding recognition. With those feelings, inseparable from them, came the vast community
of lost souls that haunted my girlhood.

I brooded for months about how to substantiate tenuous
feelings and phantom injuries without demeaning historic realities. Could I do it at all, let alone correctly, was

a question I couldn't answer. I seesawed between the ups of maybe and the downs of impossible until, one restless dawn, I grasped at a thin straw, trite for sure but a straw nonetheless: Like every human being, I have a story of my own. In part a simple one, in part a can of tangled worms. Sorting out the parts, seeing where they overlapped and how they differed, exploring my take on them, was slow going, exceedingly slow.

I had time. I had will and guarded hopes. I had ideas. So I took a deep breath and the first step, most tentatively.

I started with the facts of my story, used some fictional lumber to build them up, fumbled for ways to brace the slanted rickety construct with basics of commonality. True to characterological form, I did this covertly, initially anyhow, producing pages for my eyes only, classified documents I could bury in file drawers or shred as bungled attempts to convey the actual and the intangible stuff I was born with and retained, or acquired over the years.

Gradually, I uncovered various parts of my thickly layered story; some surprised me, others were predictable, a few were as dark and relentless as I had feared. Still, after all this time, it feels as though I have just begun to unpack my baggage. I don't yet see what remains, folded and waiting, at the bottom of it.

This much I see, have sensed since childhood, a feeling identified in that legend I read years ago: Shadows of the dead are powerful, insistent, and have a long reach. The shadows that dwell in me will never rest easy, never be revealed in the negligible light I flicker, never feel the boundless warm respect I have for them, never protect me from invasive visions of the evil that made them everlasting shadows. The thought I give them will never be enough. Even so, I won't let go of what they give me, on loan only, an immeasurable thing, the hold of their absence.

Step by Step

I babysat one winter when I was in high school. Our class needed to raise money for a trip to Gettysburg in April, and the lower-school office had a list of parents who needed occasional sitters. A Mrs. Fast was on the list. She was, the secretary told me, Mrs. Howard Fast. I knew Howard Fast was a famous author, but that was all I knew about him the evening I went to the ground-floor apartment off Central Park West on 67th Street, or it might have been 68th. If my parents had known anything about him and his politics, they would have stopped me from breezing into what I quickly realized was a potentially unsafe situation.

Mr. Fast introduced me to his two children who were playing a rowdy game of Slapjack on the dining-room table. Then he took me into his study. His voice was low and solemn as he told me not to answer the phone or to make calls, never to open the door to anyone, not the doorman or super, not a policeman or deliveryman, not my friends who might want to pass the time with me, nobody, never! I almost quit on the spot, but then I thought: An adventure, payment, why not? Almost sixteen, I was long on ennui, short of excitement.

There was a television set in the living room. Mr. Fast showed me how to angle the rabbit ears to get comparatively unsnowy reception. Then he left, double-locking the three locks on the front door from the outside. Locking me in, it felt like, and convincing me that the metal gates I noticed on the windows were not necessarily a standard feature of living on the street level. I didn't meet Mrs. Fast, she was on a trip, I was told. I remember silently vowing not to tell my parents about Mr. Fast's instructions. I knew they wouldn't let me take that job a second time.

When the kids were asleep, I went into the study and sat at the desk. I opened the single unlocked drawer and looked for a clue to the strict and scary warnings Mr. Fast gave me. I found nothing but sheets and pads of paper, envelopes, stamps, paper clips, a dozen or so cheerfully yellow Dixon Ticonderoga No. 2 pencils, already sharpened. Then I inspected the titles of the books on the shelves; no obvious clues there either. There was a row of Mr. Fast's books, one about Thomas Paine. I skimmed some of their pages, couldn't find anything that suggested he might be a candidate for dire threats. I wasn't watching a Hitchcock movie on the Fast's erratic television set, but I felt jolts of fear when the phone I couldn't answer rang, when the backfire of a car in the street sent jitters racing through me, when

I heard the tumblers of the locks turning and wasn't sure who would come through the door. Thankfully, it was Mr. Fast, home before 11:30, as promised. I thought about asking him what he was afraid of, but refrained. I told him the children were adorable, they hadn't given me any trouble, the phone rang twice, and said yes, gladly, when he asked if I would babysit again sometime.

In school the next day, I got the "lowdown," as she called it, from our math teacher. Howard Fast was more than merely a fellow traveler, she informed me, he was an important and notably vocal member of the Communist Party in the United States, briefly imprisoned after his resolutely uncooperative appearance before the House Un-American Activities Committee a few years previously, and presently blacklisted. I knew about the HUAC's powerful and twisted reach, how it uncoiled like a rattlesnake to instantly terrify and poison anyone, including people who were falsely accused or others who were purposefully minding their own business. Still, I resolved to continue working for a person with the publicly demonstrated courage of his convictions, as long as those beliefs weren't illegal, cruel, amoral, idiotic, or otherwise objectionable.

I wasn't asked to babysit for the Fasts again. I sat for another family three times, added my earnings to the class fund, and wept at Gettysburg, thinking of so many lives lost fighting for a few low hills, ridges, and knolls.

The phrase "fellow traveler" came to mind when I happened to think about why I resist traveling, which jogged my memory of the one-episode thriller of a job I had decades ago, and now tugs me back to looking at my reluctance to take trips.

Reluctance is putting it mildly. For a person with millennia of diaspora embedded in her genetic material, I am seriously averse to journeying. I do it occasionally, on relatively short trips with a longstanding travel companion: my husband. Over the years, I have seen a bit of the world, enough to know how little I know about its peoples and places. A little is something. Despite the varied languages, customs, climates, politics, religions, and landscapes that people live in and with, humankind's intrinsic commonality bolsters my empirical impression that a nearby part can stand for the far-flung whole.

This may be too simplistic a view of our highly complex species on our widely diversified planet, but the older I get, the more reductive my thinking is, and not for lack of curiosity. Time is not a renewable resource at any age, and at mine it is approaching scarcity. I try to conserve it by narrowing my sights and involvements, but trying isn't accomplishing. All too often I waste irretrievable days and my attention on marginal matters, pass hours with people I don't enjoy seeing, cling to recurring recollections, spend hours on fuzzy wool-gathering or dead-end digressions. A week may elapse before I grab hold of my notional blue pencil and temporarily unclutter what I can of life as I know it.

I wonder how many people who grew up with computers know what blue-penciling means. If I told them Occam's razor was my handheld go-to simplifying device, they might think I was a switchblade-wielding old gang girl. A rapid search on their little multifunction gadgets could set them straight. I use a number of smart machines for their convenience, abundance of information, and speedy recall capabilities, but I balk at the prospect of machines making larger and maybe irreversible inroads on human brainwork and its rewards, on humanity in general.

These days, I balk at many innovations and unfamiliar situations that I used to take in brisk stride. I am still sure-footed, but something interrupts my forward motion. I suspect it might be my sense of a broad deep chasm between populations that could, should overlap if not intertwine. There were always conspicuous and wholly appropriate generation gaps, but the present-day distance between native citizens of the digital world and people whose origins are in a pre-computer culture seems more like a rupture than a gap. We can handle the new online technology, but it's not inherently ours, not our formative method of acquiring, storing, and retrieving knowledge, making and contacting friends, finding jobs, medical advice, love, shoes, directions, furniture, bowling balls, hotels, shower curtains, just about every big or little thing or thought that is findable. We are goggle-eyed tourists in the global nation of cyberspace. At heart, we know it's not home, we don't belong there.

Traipsing through the immense digital ecosystem and its virtual realities is one thing, and being an actual tourist is another thing. Even when the scenery wows me, even where I understand the language, the distinct differences of every location unsettle me, intensify my lifelong feeling of being out of place, anywhere. That feeling is, on several levels, my origin story, a story many immigrants and refugees have and know in their bones for a generation, at the least. It might also be an inducement, my excuse perhaps, to stay put. Why travel to experience my same old story? I don't believe it is worth a journey, to borrow a sightsee-rating from the Michelin guidebooks.

My disinclination to globetrot results in my missing out on most of the world's wondrous and engaging particulars, but I can live with that, given the wonders in walking distance. If my observation about people everywhere being innately similar is credible, then it follows that sticking in the mud of a small area can reveal a bigger picture. This statement may dishonor the laws of logic as taught in college philosophy courses, but speaking anecdotally, as a regular pedestrian in a metropolis, it holds up.

Walking is more than a way to go somewhere. People walk solo or accompanied for many reasons, among them recreation, romance, fitness, contemplation, to bodily enter and be part of a natural or man-made landscape, to join political protests, religious pilgrimages, fundraising walkathons and celebratory parades, to relieve stress, on journeys of self or cultural or sexual or spiritual discovery, to attempt eccentric or record-setting feats that may be undertaken for the Warholian incentive of a fifteen-minute media-blink of fame, to pursue their careers as pickpockets or photographers, to test and possibly prove their endurance on long-distance treks, for botanizing, hiking, birdwatching. All of that and more aside, the physical activity of taking one step after another often energizes a conceptual machine shop where projects, ideas, emotions, speeches, plans, arguments, daily logistics and the like can be sorted, shaped, repaired, polished, or junked. Many people take their mind for a walk before they begin many different kinds of work, according to biographies, memoirs, and essays I read over the years, and a sizable number of contemporary and past composers, scholars, writers, artists, and scientists credit walking's influence on their creative springboards. Owning a dog could be a plus, turning an obligatory outing into a dual-purpose stroll.

I never had a dog, but an early morning walk has been my workday routine for many years. Using a treadmill in a gym might be similarly helpful, but I like being outdoors. My several routes in Central Park and on streets near it are more or less fixed, their start times and durations are flexible, depending on daylight, weather, and my intermittent sciatica. Sometimes I talk aloud as I walk, mouth off with accusations and criticisms I wouldn't deliver in person, move that fractious stuff out of my mind, for a while at least; my audible aggravation used to draw stares from other walkers and joggers before the advent of mobile phones and their hands-free gizmos that have made private business public. Most days, I walk silently, listening for internal whispers and echoes. I amble or tromp or plod, the gait and pace don't matter, it's the rhythmic repetition of breath and step that gets the cadence of a sentence going or a fragment of one, a new idea or a rewording of something already written. That's enough to start with. I intone it quietly while heading for my workroom, or decide to discard it. Too many of my morning walks lead to nothing but disappointment and a dose of fresh air; I sit at my desk anyhow.

Walking is an important part of my working hours, but the larger and harder part is sitting. My final year in college I had an advisor who was then a newly published young poet and is now a grand very old man of American letters. By the time I was a senior I had forgiven him for the F he gave me in English 100 that freshman were required to take. He did that because, he explained, "You need to shake hands with failure." Even so, he raised my grade to a pass after I wept in his office.

"I have a little present for you," he said the week I graduated. "This is for sticking your butt to the chair." He chuckled as he handed me a bottle of Elmer's glue. He must have seen something in me that I didn't recognize for many years, when I decided to glue myself to a chair on a routine basis. At present, my sitting power runs out after three or so hours. If I were a hen, I'd be a poor brooder.

In the afternoons, my walks are less goal-specific, less blinkered, I should say. I go out in the city, usually alone but always in the company of other pedestrians on New York's lively streets, a few I know or recognize as neighborhood regulars, most I never saw before. Being on bustling sidewalks is a relief, almost a fiesta, after the necessary seclusion of my mornings. I buy groceries, go to a pharmacy, hardware store, library, dry cleaner, bakery, wherever an errand or appointment or whim may take me, all the while relishing the sociable and sensory gumbo of voices, faces, colors, window displays, diverting incidents, clothing, chance encounters, the random cacophony of traffic, the familiar looking strange on some days. I generally circulate on foot, uptown, both west and east sides, but when I take a bus or the subway, my eyes do the legwork. I stand or sit in bumper-to-bumper crowds of fellow passengers whose appearances can convey, and often do, a fleeting glimpse of their histories, enough to start me speculating about the lives temporarily in my field of vision. My stop arrives, signaling an end to guesswork while in transit.

I am a pedestrian by habit, residential circumstance, inclination, and for occupational assistance. Still, the word puzzles me. A pedestrian is a walker. Alternatively, the word describes a person or idea or activity or object as commonplace and boring. I fail to see a connection between traveling by foot and the dull or ordinary. On the contrary, walking stretches minds along with muscles, grounds you in the surroundings, impels both close attention and wider reflection that can change outlooks or spark invention, and may lead to all sorts of extraordinary accomplishments by people you might not particularly notice on urban sidewalks, rural roads and trails, or circling the corridors of suburban malls.

A high-speed online query and response would likely clarify the baffling discrepancy in the word "pedestrian." Instead of keyboarding a search, I will saunter a mile of city blocks to the library I use, consult the big, solid, and authoritative *Oxford English Dictionary* for variant usages of the word, see if the mystery can be solved, to my satisfaction anyhow. I might stop at a coffee shop I like, chat with the waitress I know who works the weekday afternoon shift behind the counter, admire a snapshot or cellphone video of her teenage gymnast daughter performing on the uneven parallel bars. Such a companionable moment is also a satisfaction; others may be found on the way from here to there.

Sounding the Territory

person I hadn't thought of in decades sprang to mind recently with the zing of an arrow released from a bow. I was waiting for a bus on Lexington Avenue, headed downtown to a movie. There was no one else at the bus stop. The bus arrived, the doors opened, the driver glanced at me and, suddenly, the bus kneeled. Me? Old? Visibly past my prime? I stared at that lowered step, then I glared daggers at the driver, and then I boarded the bus remembering: Looking her age never fazed Mrs. Exeter.

When I was a girl reading magazines for clues to the mysterious enterprise of adulthood, I admired Mrs. Exeter. "Mrs. Exeter" was a generic term coined by *Vogue* in the early 1950s to denote women of a certain age, loosely reckoned as verging on sixty, who, despite their advanced years, were still in step with fashion. Mrs. Exeter's age

group probably comprised the bulk of *Vogue's* reader-
ship, although she was usually relegated to a column of
text at the back of the magazine under the heading of
"Mrs. Exeter's List," indicating the page number of the
clothes pictured on younger slimmer models that might
be appropriate garments for fuller figures. I have a dim,
maybe false, memory of occasionally seeing Mrs. Exeter
on a picture page of her own, photographed with her
putative friends in seated positions, perhaps to conceal
the spread that ordinarily reshaped mature women's hips
in the years before exercise workouts, faddish weight-
loss diets, dextroamphetamine pills, and liposuction
became popular weapons in the fight against nature and
flab. Stately, plumpish Mrs. Exeter and her friends were
reportedly busy with charitable works, ate in swanky restaurants wearing hats that swooped precariously close to
a soup spoon's path, gave dainty tea parties for debutante
nieces at Christmastime, and frequently vacationed in
winter and summer beach resorts, but never ever wore
sleeveless dresses, open-toed shoes, or swimsuits without
a mid-calf bathing coat covering them.

Vogue scrapped Mrs. Exeter, rather unmercifully I felt,
at the start of the 1960s, when the advertising industry embraced a dubious gospel that heralded youth and
tasteful nudity as key factors in the mass movement of
consumer goods; this despite the postwar baby boom that
would inexorably result in a larger elderly population
than existed previously. But before Mrs. Exeter was banished from *Vogue* if not from demographic fact, I admired
her. I didn't particularly care for the high-society life she

led. It was her aplomb that appealed. She was comfortable with herself, vibrantly in tune with her matronly body and situation. In that respect, I thought Mrs. Exeter might be a better model than the pouty wraith-like nymphets who chased her off *Vogue's* slick pages.

To my surprise and delight, Mrs. Exeter has made a comeback, as I coincidentally learned the other day when flipping through *Vogue* in a periodontist's waiting room. There she was again, soon after I remembered her when the bus kneeled; chance, pure happenstance, dumb luck, for once those unpredictable engines appeared to be running on my timetable. I was glad to see that Mrs. Exeter didn't just outlast her years of exile and enter the new millennium, but was also promoted to the magazine's View pages under the Style Council banner with a subhead of "Ask Mrs. Exeter." She is now an arbiter of elegance for older women, making direct and thoughtful pronouncements, a distinct upgrade from her former job, and a triumph of statistics over sexiness.

Recalling Mrs. Exeter has jogged other memories of those years when I used magazines as investigative equipment. Nancy Drew had her trusty flashlight, I had *Look*, *Life*, *Time*, *The New Yorker*, *Commentary*, *Vogue*, *The Saturday Review*, *National Geographic*, *Cue*, *Fortune*, *Esquire*, *Art News*, *Harper's*, *Flair*, for a while, and *The Nation*. This sizable fleet of magazines flew through my parents' home, arriving and departing on schedule, every week or once a month. The top of a sturdy side table in our living room was reserved for magazines. Each issue was kept until its successor was delivered with the mail, at which time, read or not, it was discarded. Only *National Geographic* had a longer stay in our house; my brother stashed it in his closet so he could examine bare breasts at his leisure. I used to leaf though many of these magazines, but the three that I concentrated on, that I needed, were *Life*, *The New Yorker*, and *Vogue*.

As I attended a hard-line progressive school that categorically rejected the traditionally structured study of geography, history, science, and what were then called civics and hygiene, the latter a fifties code word for sex education, I turned to *Life* for visual instruction in those and some other subjects. *Life* showed me spacious horizons in remote places like Iceland, the African veldt, and Tierra del Fuego. I saw the crowded streets of Calcutta, Naples, and Cairo, the despair of GIs on Pork Chop Hill, the inside of a bus in Montgomery, Sing Sing on the day of the Rosenbergs' executions. I peered into Congressional corridors and sessions of the House Un-American Committee, the seedpods of flowers, gazed at the chambers of the heart and the passageways of the birth canal. I could explore these informative sights, stroll through them, taking my time. At the movies, images sped by, quicker than thought. Still photographs idled quietly on a page, waiting for someone to enter their stories, or not to. For me, a child in a family that fled from Hitler's Europe to cosmopolitan Manhattan, *Life* was America, the real whole big thing. Touring the photos in *Life*, I learned about Town Meetings in New England, Revivalists' tents pitched in the Southern pinewoods, Midwestern bake-offs, and the fat city-state of California, where everything shimmered with possibility. *Life* gave me secondhand but enticing views of the country I hoped truly to call home someday.

Equally intriguing were views of another nature: outlooks. For positional training I went to *The New Yorker* every week. It spotlighted an Anglophile-Ivy-Establishment arena that was as foreign to my experience as hot rodding on a highway in Texas, and it had a voice I aspired to then. Purveyor of cool, *The New Yorker's* prose demonstrated something my mother liked to remind me of, although her context was usually a different one, having to do with my fresh mouth. "*C'est le ton qui fait la musique,*" she frequently told me. *Ton* mattered, and *le bon ton* topped it. I could see that in *The New Yorker's* articles, short stories, profiles, reviews, and advertisements, even when I had trouble getting a message lurking below the polished *ton* or when, worse, I found the cartoons unfunny. Because I lived in New York City, I felt I had a citizen's right to the sophistication that pulsed in every line of text, and often between the lines, on *The New Yorker's* pages. Even the typeface, which I later learned was called sans serif, impressed me. It projected a bedrock devotion to restraint. No messy twisty excesses ornamented either the ideas or their appearance in print in *The New Yorker*. Smart, spare, mildly acid, reliably correct: That was the way to think and to be; at the very least, it had to look as if you had those qualities. When you got the stylish skin down pat, the substance would probably fill it. That was one of many mistakes I made at the time.

Vogue I read for practical tips. They were couched in honey-tongued imperatives that steered women through the currents of allure's narrow straits. Unfaltering attention to hair, hems, nails, makeup, the cunning use of colorful accessories to refresh last season's outfits or tired home decor, romantic candlelight dinners with hard-working husbands, and charming rapport with everyone else, were emphatically advised. Following this advice didn't guarantee a passage to attractiveness, but it was an approach. If you did everything *Vogue* urged you to do, you might just wind up looking okay and feeling good about yourself, your near and dear, your appeal to the world at large.

The problem with *Vogue*, for me, was its fashion pages. The photographs were too fantastic, severely arty or glaringly flashy or plain implausible. The models, both professional and society beauties, and the occasional actress or ballet dancer or royal, were mostly flawless, svelte and glossy as white egrets, their clothes flapping in breezes I couldn't feel. They were often pictured in sporting activities, gesturing with an ease that implied years of practice on tennis courts, ski slopes, and golf courses, years which, along with athletic skills, I did not have. The women in *Vogue* bore little resemblance to the ones I saw in *Life*, at home, in school and on the streets, in life itself. Nobody cried in *Vogue*, no black or yellow or brown models appeared on its pages in that bluntly noninclusive era, no upper arms or thighs bulged lumpily, nobody slapped a bratty child, nobody worried about anything at all or was bored or lonely or afraid or sick in *Vogue*'s dreamy version of reality. Mrs. Exeter was the only woman in *Vogue* who seemed genuine to me, and she was an outright invention.

Evoking my magazine-reading past, recollecting my adolescent hunger for illuminating clues to a fast-looming future, has led me, willy-nilly, to think about something else, someone else. Mrs. Exeter's graceful aging may have been the ostensible point of the arrow that struck me at the bus stop, but the actual and timelier point is a different one. I have crossed the numerical divide that *Vogue* established for Mrs. Exeter, and there are fewer futures open to me now, one of them being the alarming prospect of my father's final years. I know that familial history doesn't always repeat itself, but the dreadful fact is: DNA stacks the deck.

I don't have even tentative answers to the large hard questions posed by prolonged dementia. I have only a handful of observations about my father's experience. This is anecdotal information, unscientific for sure, weighted by affection and close involvement, skewed by my ingrained narrative bent. Narrow and sketchy as these particulars are, they may anyhow put a face on flat formidable generality. Moreover, personalizing an all-too-common affliction may in some small way defuse my fear of it, or so I hope.

My father forgot how to think, to talk, to button his shirt, to whistle, to laugh, to chew and swallow routinely; by the end, a Parkinsonian dementia of the Alzheimer type had stripped him of even the simplest bodily habits he'd had since early childhood. It took eight years for the end to arrive, and all that while his mind was draining its essential reservoirs of comprehension and knowledge. It took too long. He was a legendarily punctual person. Traffic might be at a standstill, nor'easters could blow, any number of delaying events could occur and he somehow managed to be where he had arranged to be, on the dot. He would certainly have scolded tardy death if he could have, said something like: Inconsiderate bum! Keeping me waiting!

We—my mother, her four middle-aged children, their spouses, nine grandchildren—were also waiting, restively on occasion, for my father's ordeal to conclude. We felt guilty about our impatience, but shame was overridden by the onerous realities of cognitive disinte-gration. We had a clear picture of the tough times ahead if my father lived much longer. Even so, we couldn't alter the picture, intervene in any way, help him escape his misfortune.

It would have been a different picture if my father had needed surgery or chemotherapy, or was on life-support machinery in a medical setting. No heroic measures, we would have told the doctors. Pull the plug. Do not resus-citate. But that was not and never became the case. He was in fair health for his age, eighty-four at the start of his irreversible slide into florid dementia. His Parkinson's was controlled by medication, his appetite was hearty, his cheeks were rosy, his eyes were on speaking terms with the world. Apart from enfeebled legs and a disorganizing mind, his vital systems did their customary jobs until the last year of his overlong trial by dementia. Like millions of otherwise well people ravaged by dementing disorders, my father was not in a hospital where suffering can be cut short by compassionate neglect or more hands-on pro-cedures. The demented stay home, or in long-term care facilities, enduring, often against their wishes. Unable to speak out for themselves or make common cause, they are a powerless hidden multitude whose everyday agonies seldom get even a mention in any of the heated public debates about our badly broken healthcare system, the bioethical dilemmas created by end-of-life decisions, or the Social Security catastrophe that is waiting to happen.

Dementia is a word that covers a lot of ground, most of it wasteland. Broadly speaking, it is a condition, a cluster of symptoms, few of them currently treatable. Syndrome, progressive disorder, organic brain disease, cognitive disfunction, infirmity, whichever: It is usually considered a management problem, not a medical one. That is true, and it is also false. Severe dementia is a mortal injury to the distinctive features of human life. My father's brain stabbed his mind in the back and it bled uncontrollably, bled memory, language, logic, personality, pride and will, dignity, courage, humor, hope. All we could do was watch him vanish piecemeal, erode, so slowly, to dust.

Death was constantly on my father's impaired mind. He wished to die several years before the fact. He said so, frankly, when he could word his thoughts. He was more than ready, he'd had a long full life, and he deplored his diminished state. In his lucid moments, he was sorely aware of his mental confusion, and by turns irate, agitated, sad, frightened, humiliated, and apologetic about the brand-new and frustrating stupidity that massive memory losses imposed on a formerly sharp-witted person. Somewhere inside the tangles and plaques in his brain, somewhere he could not reach handily or at all, was the man he used to be: astute, courteous, unassuming, short-tempered, firmly fair and square, a bon vivant with a zest for pranks and a gift for friendship, dutiful, a voracious reader, a should-have-been scientist quietly miserable in the family diamond business, multilingual, an intrepid traveler with often-told tales from far and wide. We tried to remind him, and ourselves,

of that worldly person by asking for stories from his
deep past, cuing him with pertinent words or phrases:
Jo'burg, Pelikaanstraat, Kuala Lumpur, Madame X in Rio,
the Savoy Grill in London, bicycling in Knokke. His
memory's inventory control system worked on a last-
in, first-out plan; when he talked about people and
events in places he had been a half-century or longer
ago, his search for words was less labored, and his
sentences were whole and cogent enough, though not
always sequential. He could usually be distracted from
regrets about his confusion by his own yarns, but his
anger was harder to deflect. Chocolate bars and ice
cream calmed him, sometimes. We were lucky, we
knew, his sort of Alzheimer's wasn't explosive or
clamorous or restlessly hyperactive, his behavior was
only occasionally chaotic, and only during the early
years of his cognitive decline.

The burden of caring for a dementing person at home
fell chiefly on my mother's elderly shoulders. Live-
in help gave her brief daily respites from the constant
effort and vigilance that burden demands, but did not
begin to lighten it emotionally. Even so, she would
not put my father into an institution of any kind,
although she didn't have the satisfaction of knowing that
he knew he was home. He was utterly and intractably
convinced that he lived in a hotel, an amazingly exact
replica of the apartment that he and my mother had
occupied for almost all of their years in America. The

view of Central Park was the same, he admitted as we wheeled his chair around the apartment to show him that it was home, the rooms were identical in size and layout, the furniture was the same, yes, those were his clothes in the closets and bureaus, but the place was definitely not home: "You can't fool me, goddammit!"

The hotel was in various locations, always at some unspecified distance from New York, and even in bright daylight my father was acutely anxious about getting home before dark. When he had the words, he begged us for money, "a couple of twenties, don't be a piker," for a taxi to take him home. You are home, we said, trust us, you're already where you want to be, you don't need a taxi. He couldn't believe us, his delusion was unshakable. We gave him the money anyway, in dollar bills, thinking that a wad of cash in his pocket might make him feel he was still independent, in charge of his acts, thoughts, and finances. He promptly gave the money away, to the door-men, to people he saw on streets when he was wheeled outdoors on nice days, to anyone who happened to cross his habitually generous path.

Long-standing habits die hard. His love of reading out-lasted his ability to make sense of words on paper. Now my father read books and magazines upside-down as often as not. Or he pored over the Manhattan telephone directory, one torn-out page at a time, randomly search-ing for names he might recognize, and jot on a note for our future use the names of friends and business acquaintances who should be informed of his death when it occurred so they would not miss his funeral. He had attended many of their funerals, we sometimes reminded him: It didn't seem right to us, mentioning those deaths, reducing the crowd he expected and deserved to have at his funeral service.

My father had been a businessman since the age of nineteen, and he continued to go to the office every morning. After breakfast, he would get dressed, with assistance, and be eager to leave for work. His office was my brother's room refurnished as a den, and his desk was a shopping bag crammed with slips of paper that he consulted constantly. He was always a list maker; his lists had lists of their own, wee memos he kept in his shirt pocket. His note-making habit persisted although his handwriting became largely illegible, typically Parkinsonian, cramped meandering script that resembled snail slime, the visible residue of meaning but not meaning itself. He wrote his notes on paper, on his trousers with his index finger, some scrawled in the air, many having to do with his wished-for death. His undecipherable scribbles often had one capital letter standing out, an M. It took us a while to come up with an explanation, possibly erroneous, for that M: It was the initial letter of his burial society's name. "Guard this with your life," he told me one day, explicit instructions after a half-hour of incoherent speech. He handed me a tightly folded piece of Kleenex. I unfolded it and saw a lonely inky M on it.

I made a production of putting the tissue in my purse, in a zippered compartment. He was pleased to see that I took his request seriously.

Or did M stand for mama? A child's cry?

One of my father's habitual traits changed radically during the years he slogged through the self-parching desert of dementia. Apart from having liked to reminisce about his adventures in exotic lands, he had never been a big talker, not at home. Not that he would have gotten a word in edgewise, my mother could talk the paint off walls, and we four children made more than our fair share of gab. In the event, my father was by nature a quiet person, a listener, reflective, defensively silent at times, merely preoccupied at others, nose in a book, head in who-knows-where, a faraway kingdom of secrets, I believed when I was a girl. Dementia turned my father into an industrial-strength yakker. It seemed as though he felt compelled to make up for a lifetime of characteristic reticence. There were days when he chattered nonstop and most of what he said escaped us—we caught only a phrase here, a word there. Other days, or when he told his deep-time tales we had heard before, we could more or less follow his wandering mind on its fitful zigzag route through eight decades and five continents and seven languages, those we spoke at least.

He also used the telephone in his ongoing struggle for verbal connectedness. My father made a lot of calls, farewell calls for the most part, many to people whose

numbers he remembered although he forgot they were
dead. He recalled numbers better than names and words,
not only phone numbers but street addresses, birthdays,
business figures, and mileage between cities throughout
the world. He was hard-of-hearing, selectively, we often
thought, but didn't like to wear his hearing aid, and
when he made those calls he may have thought that, as
usual, he was just not catching the voices of his friends
and relatives. He didn't say much on the phone, he
mainly listened, but he enjoyed using it, making dozens
of calls an hour if no one unjacked the telephone on a
shelf next to his easy chair in the den, or even if they
did. For four years, he was the wheezy breather on my
answering machine; he never identified himself, seldom
left a message, and when he did it was: Emergency here,
call me. Or words to that effect.

He watched television for hours on end, but what he saw
may have been something other than the sights on the
screen. He invariably pressed the mute button. My father
handled the remote-control device as though he'd grown
up with electronic gadgets, switching channels fast and
deftly, switching, switching, never finding the program
he seemed to be looking for, and whatever that was he
would not or could not say.

Apart from imaginary shows he might have been
watching on television, he occasionally had authentic
visual hallucinations. For a while, early on in the course
of his cognitive disorder, my father believed he was

witnessing crimes being committed, robberies, vicious muggings, murders. He wanted to prevent the crimes but couldn't because of his weak legs, his lame brain, his this, his that, a garbled litany of helplessness. For a solid week, he repeatedly maintained that there was a corpse on the floor in the living room. Loosely interpreted, what he said was: There, there, under the piano, goddammit! Plain as day. What's wrong with your eyes? Don't tell the officials or I'll wind up in court.

He was already sentenced, doing hard time. We rolled up the Chinese rug on the chance that his gruesome hallucination might have been fueled by his staring at its sinister design of fierce-looking fire-breathing coiled dragons. We supposed, foolishly in all likelihood, that there was still some symmetry of image and idea in his deteriorating mind. However, the corpse did disappear several days later. The muggings continued for a few more weeks.

In the belief that socialization might slightly decelerate his slippage, we enrolled my father in an Alzheimer's group that met on Wednesdays at a nearby synagogue. This was in the third year of his losing battle with his brain. He was reluctant to go, but agreed to try it if I would take him there, and promise to stay in the room with him. The first morning we went, there wasn't a ramp on the five steps up to the front door, making it almost impossible for me to push his wheelchair with him in it through that door. I chided myself for not checking out the place beforehand, it wasn't suitable for people who couldn't manage stairs. The building's superintendent happened to be outside and saw our predicament. He told us that the wooden ramp usually on the steps was broken and had not yet been replaced, but he knew what to do. He lifted the trapdoors of the freight elevator that rose from the basement to the sidewalk, and wheeled my father onto the clanky metal platform of that elevator. Once inside, they could take the passenger elevator to the third-floor meeting room. The super wouldn't let me ride the freight elevator, for reasons of insurance liability, he explained, although he kindly overlooked that constraint to get my father where he had to go. I pried my father's fingers off my wrist, he was gripping me like a vise, and I tried to reassure him that he'd be okay, this stranger taking him away was a friendly person, a helper. Watching my father descend below ground level, shouting, terrified, angry, I thought: This is a dress rehearsal that nobody needs.

I took him to that group seven or eight times. I knew that my father and I wouldn't last long there. I burst into tears one morning when I heard a man in his sixties despairingly confess to shaving his teeth by mistake. My father insisted on accompanying me to the ladies' room when I wanted to splash water on my swollen eyes. "You go, I go, it's a deal," he said, and he was right, we had a deal, though I hadn't figured on toilet togetherness. He wouldn't have used a restroom anyhow, he wore adult diapers whenever he left home. Soon, he would wear them day and night. He was not the only person in that group with continence problems, there was a whiff of urine in the air, along with the sweet scent of talcum powder: essence of infants. Perhaps my father smelled the piss and found it offensive. He vehemently refused to stay for the lunch periods, waving away the sandwiches and grapes I brought along for both of us. He complained that everyone in the group was too old, too silly, too rude, too boring, too weird. He was by several years the senior member of that sorry club. His behavior was not the weirdest, not noticeably anyhow.

As the years passed, he recognized only the most familiar faces, people he saw every few days, although he confused our names when he didn't lose them. When visitors came, less and less frequently, as happens with visits to chronic shut-ins or to the demented, who are stigmatized like so many people with various mental diseases, the identity of those rare visitors eluded my father entirely. For all he knew, they might have been aliens from outer space, and many times that is exactly what he believed those old friends were. Paranoia often comes with dementia's territory, and my father's took the form of a rigid conviction that a Great Spymaster in the Sky had marked him for constant surveillance, cloak-and-dagger work carried out by an extraterrestrial police force that could operate on earth. Was the celestial overseer an allusion to God? Was the alien police force a haunting flashback to the inhumanity of the Nazis? Could metaphor still enter and cross his mind?

Or did we lean on stray vague hints for even a semblance of explanatory relief? Whatever the answers, they didn't translate to useful.

The firm certainty that interplanetary spies were watching him didn't particularly scare my father, but it did obsess him for weeks at a time. He insisted that airplanes, birds in flight, clouds, the moon, were not what they seemed, they were hovering camouflaged spaceships with telescopes and cameras and listening equipment pointed at him. Sometimes the alien peepers and eavesdroppers sent him important messages, he could hear them shouting loudly through megaphones. He was sad to say, clearly or in scrambled words, that he couldn't understand the announcements because they were made in a language he didn't know. My father's perseveration about outer-space espionage was comic, and it wasn't.

He always loved to eat, whether in fine restaurants, at an Automat, or snagging pickled herrings from a barrel on Essex Street. Maître d's in cities all over the globe greeted my father warmly, he was an appreciative loyal customer and a princely tipper. He had a tenacious on-again, off-again weight problem, but that never hampered his enjoyment of food and its convivial rituals. He wasn't a greedy eater, stuffing some implacable inmost emptiness, he ate quite delicately, cutlery held just so, silver ribbons fluttering above and around his plate. In the fifth year of his mental disintegration, my father began to eat air,

invisible spoonful after spoonful, his hand moving repet-
itively, unerringly, toward his slightly open mouth. He
didn't swallow the air, but kept spooning it in as though it
came from a puzzlingly bottomless bowl of mulligatawny,
his favorite soup.

Approaching the final stretch of his long ordeal, my father
retired from such business of life as was still left to him.
He grew more and more silent, and one rainy afternoon
ceased to talk at all. He seemed stunned, stone-faced, a
fossil of his formerly animated being. We could see anxiety in his blue eyes, and nothing else there, nothing
recognizable. Dementia had done its cruel worst, dispos-
sessing my father of self-memory, of cultural freight and
experiential lore, of human life's most human attribute:
the natural gift of language. Were words still there, whirling like tumbleweed across the barrens of his mind? Or
did language vanish with his lost personhood?
    I can hardly imagine the magnitude of my father's
numerous losses, the holes in his brain formed by the
deaths of clusters of neurons, blank spaces responsible
for the disturbing enigmas and novelties he must have
encountered every moment, mysteries of time and
motion, of cause and effect, of place and person, of ordinary things and events, of you and I, hello and goodbye, of
shoes, headache, thunderclap, soap, and orange juice, an
entire universe of strange stuff accosting him constantly,
fresh raw data he could not process, much less retain,
every dawn a perplexing new start he did not want. I

wonder if he ever had the feeling of being buried alive, trapped in a lonely box of bones and skin, of involuntary duration. I wonder if he cared, or was he beyond loneliness by then, beyond emotional, moral, and temporal awareness, beyond even his own desolate wilderness of incomprehension, feeling only, maybe, sensory stimuli: a kiss, the heat of the day, salt in his mouth.

He died in his sleep, at home, a week before his ninety-second birthday.

There was a big crowd at my father's funeral, just as he wanted and expected. Along with the planned speakers, several people spontaneously rose to eulogize him. Everyone spoke of him with affection, some humorously, some with plangent nostalgia in their reminiscences, others with gratitude for the help that my father was characteristically eager to give, and did give, to every needy person, school, hospital, and charitable organization that appealed to him for assistance. All those speeches and not a word, not one word, not a hint or a whisper, nothing but a crushing silence about what mattered most for eight long years, to him, his family, his friends, his vast community of fellow sufferers.

At the cemetery later that morning, the rabbi's chant was punctuated by the drumming of a woodpecker looking for lunch in a nearby oak. *Yisgadal*, rat-a-tat, *v'yiskadash*, rat-a-tat. Glancing up, I spotted the bird making that unseemly noise. I scowled at the clattering intruder because I couldn't shout or clap to shoo it away. Then I thought: Is this a message? From him? An appeal in rudimentary Morse dotted and dashed on a lush leafy tree of life? Heads up, people, rat-a-tat, this matters, rat-a-tat, get cracking, goddammit, it's time to make a racket about dementia. The rabbi continued to chant the Kaddish, evidently unfazed by the disturbance; it must happen frequently, given the trees in most cemeteries. I meant to ask him about that when the graveside service was over, but I forgot.

There: incomplete, slanted, notional but there: expressed. "A momentary stay against confusion," as a poet said, as I feel this is, a little spoke in fear's wheel, for a little while.

Ripple Effects

ne of New York City's notable attractions is the Guggenheim Museum. Crowds of tourists and New Yorkers flock to see Frank Lloyd Wright's stunning building and the art in it. Across Fifth Avenue and one block north of the museum is an entrance to Central Park that leads to the jogging track around another of Manhattan's notable sights: the Reservoir, a 106-acre artificial lake. It was formerly used to receive and distribute water to Manhattan residents, and is now an urban treasure. The city's midtown and uptown buildings that rise above the park's trees appear to be floating in the sky over scenic views of foliage or bare branches around a beautiful lake with a variety of aquatic birds on it, feeding, socializing, imprinting offspring. People visiting the Guggenheim often include a stop at the Reservoir to gaze at this dazzling wide-open vista in a densely built and congested metropolis, and they generally congregate near the area of the track reached from the 90th Street entrance to the park. Countless videos and photos, mostly selfies these days, are taken from that popular vantage point, and large numbers of them are sent to distant friends and relatives, posted on social media sites, photoshopped perhaps. In the background of those pictures, directly across the water on Central Park West, is the building I grew up in. I often wonder where in the world those incidentally captured images of my family home have traveled, and who has looked at all those people, every one of them unique, all posed in front of my background: my origins; a milieu; my upbringing; a particular set of circumstances.

Which isn't to say that anyone else sees what I would see in their pictures.

I like to walk before sitting at my desk for hours, and the track around the Reservoir is nearby, only one of its many features that appeal to me. My background comes to mind, willy-nilly, when I catch sight of its location as I walk. The exterior of that building is unchanged, and seeing it carries me back to what I was and still am in some ways, which can spur me to look at the now and ahead. Push or pull, that apartment house is a magnet for my eyes and thoughts.

The room that was mine has two windows facing the park. I glanced or peered at the Reservoir many times a day. As a young child, I saw that body of water as an ocean separating the Upper West Side with its pockets of Old World ambiance and its many speakers of European languages, my family among them, and the new American world and its citizens on the Upper East Side, a nation I hadn't yet explored. Once in a while, I was taken eastward to catch a Fifth Avenue bus to midtown, where my mother stalked the aisles of the two department stores that she thought sold suitable clothes for birthday party-going, velvet dresses usually, with elaborate lace collars that drooped on my shoulders as though in empathetic misery.

Some mornings, I stare at the water as if it contains a message for me, a focal point I need. It could be a face, a place, a hope, a song, a word or phrase, a goal, an idea, a recollection, a plan. I frequently look for and don't routinely find a center of attention on my routine walks.

Periodically, the water level in the basin is lowered for the easier removal of overgrown reeds, grasses, small trees, and wildflowers thriving in crannies between the riprap of boulders on the sloped wall below the railing around the basin. Although that thick flora shelters birds and their nests of young, turtles, the occasional raccoon, mice and rats, it is anyhow cut away and discarded, leaving only a patchy stubble of desiccated stems, frail tufts, and gnarled roots. When I see that nearly bare wall of stones, I often feel bereft, stripped of safety, of potential. The deeply-rooted greenery makes a comeback, on schedule, and so do the birds on their nests.

On days there are whitecaps scudding across the choppy water and I hear the wind gusting and moaning, I recall the frequently stormy weather of my adolescence, the reflexive deluge of tears followed by an onerous calm.

Sometimes the skyline around the water reminds me of the panorama of silhouetted buildings projected before the space show began in the Natural History Museum's old planetarium, and how pleased I was to know that I could sit anywhere in the large domed auditorium and always find home because our apartment house was near the Eldorado's unmistakable towers. I habitually oriented myself parochially. My school, friends, cousins, public library, doctor and dentist, the locations of my piano, ballet, riding, and Hebrew after-school lessons, my Woolworths, parentally approved movie theater, soda fountain, everything I needed, knew, and wanted was on the West Side, close by, familiar.

On bright cloudless windless days when the water is a flat silvery mirror that reflects the skyline, upside-down and in blurred detail but with the buildings aligned, it appears they have doubled their height. It is a pretty sight but it troubles me, given the city's supertall towers being built or already completed. Ever-higher out-of-human-scale buildings are likely to be the global urban future, a dispiriting prospect.

When the water is so still it seems solid, I pick up a pebble and toss it over the ornamental iron railing just to see its effect: the spreading circles of consequence that even a small thing or a person can cause.

If there is a thick fog blanketing the water and obscuring the skyline, the treetops, other people at a distance on the track, almost everything but its own dense presence, I try not to anticipate confusion heading in my direction, soon to arrive for the day, most probably in my workroom. I don't regularly succeed in thwarting it.

A circle of ducks paddling around and around in their species' courtship behavior before flying off reminds me of leaving my parental nest, not exactly a fledgling, not exactly aloft either. I married and moved across the water, an easy optional passage compared to the one my parents made across an actual ocean, fleeing Europe, deeply apprehensive about almost everything: who they left behind, why they were going, where they were headed. I was with them, their first born, an infant. I always wanted to believe they found some comfort and hope in my presence, though I was never told that, and never asked.

Often, the captivating vista prompts me to think about the vast number of people who saw and took an important part of my past with them, figuratively speaking, or deleted it, which I can't do. If it is still in their smartphones and cameras, I could be in Helsinki, Kyoto, Wichita Falls, Reykjavik, Montevideo, Kuala Lumpur, Chicago, anywhere and everywhere, unseen in person but there in pixilated imagery of my formative context. Or that image could be stored in a so-called cloud, retrievable on demand.

A person's past is always present, though retrieving it isn't always easy. It can't be packed away in trunks and crates labeled "Not Wanted on Voyage," the usual wording of a stowage possibility offered to passengers on cruise ships and ocean liners who travel with a lot of baggage. Nor can it be sent to dead storage, like furniture, files, tax records, library books, archival material, and other seldom used items, available upon request. Out of sight isn't out of mind; a personal past is in there, somewhere, active or dormant, an ongoing accreting changing reality. Short of amnesia or dementia, there is no denying its presence.

Not that I am stuck in my yesterdays but, like the turtles in the Reservoir, they surface unpredictably, some more insistently than others.

A week ago I spotted a newly installed table at my local Barnes & Noble. It had piles of books and a placard on it that announced REALISTIC FICTION. I skimmed several of the front flaps to see what that oxymoronic coupling might produce, and suddenly recalled the start of a fearsome Baba Yaga story my mother read to me long ago. It began: "There was and there was not…," a typical opening of many Eastern European fairy tales. That contradictory phrase resonates with a sigh of skepticism absent from "Once upon a time . . .," and hints at its unreliability in telling stories about love, luck, power, evil, vanity, truth, misery, terror, slyness, magic, faith, ignorance, and more.

Ever since I happened to notice that emphatic sign and remembered that loaded phrase, I have been hearing its whisper. There is and there is not an opportunity in it for me. I will or I won't turn up its volume. I should stop vacillating, take that soft rustling hint of a chance, see where it goes.

After I stopped hearing, reading, loving and dreading fairy tales of the Brothers Grimm, Anderson, Lang, Perrault, Potter et al. variety, after I inhaled the heady oxygen of romantic, heroic, adventure, and tragic stories for teen readers, after I was done with college-course textbooks, and after my young-children-at-home years, I read recreationally, as a pastime. There was no program to it, no compass either. I read novels mostly but not exclusively, with jackets or titles that caught my eye in bookstore displays and on library shelves, or I plucked possibilities from reviews, took tips from friends who were also eager readers. All those early and later years of avid reading, all those books I took in, and I never thought of myself as a squirrel, instinctively gathering food to store in the hollows and branches of my brain.

Approaching my fortieth birthday, I began to write a brief family history for my children. Unexpectedly, it became a novel. Reading shifted from a pastime to a purposeful necessity for me. The nourishment I cached in earlier years was helpful, but not enough. The more I wrote, the more I needed: words, ideas, narrative models, more secrets, insights, joys and sorrows of people I never met, landscapes and cultural lore from worlds beyond my temporal and circumstantial horizons. Occasionally, I pictured the mass of reading I did as a sort of black hole, a cold dark maw with a gravitational pull that might swallow me, land me in a place where the usual workings of words would lose their light, warmth, sense, traction. That vision is not pretty or productive, but at least it was infrequent. More often, I saw all that reading as a job I had to do in order to continue writing, a job with no pay, no insurance, no co-workers for help or distraction, few rewards, and no end in sight. However, it did amount to something.

Several decades have passed, and I am still doing that job, but differently: I don't always finish a book. My verbal and informational needs haven't changed or been fully satisfied, but time is a greater consideration for me than it used to be. I read the first forty or so pages of every book, then abandon it if those pages feel dry and windy to me, deserts where rootless tumbleweed blows aimlessly, endlessly.

Another difference is: I take notes, on paper; a couple of sentences, a word, a new view of an age-old situation, a reference to or explanation of something I didn't know about that appeals to me. I sometimes have trouble accessing details of the unrecorded foodstuff I stored in earlier years, and notetaking is a hedge against that lapse. The notes are in manila folders I can open at will, leaf through the jumbled scraps of paper until I find what I need, often not what I began to look for. I could organize the folders by topic, but I like to see the uncategorized notes bump and change the directions of their words as they collide, like dodgem cars at amusement parks.

I do and I don't write fiction these days. I don't invent characters and plot episodes that reveal or alter those people. I do write essays that are often sparked and supported by my memories.

Scientific data and theories aside, a memory could be considered a fiction of the mind, a construct shaped by a person's learned, retained, and recalled visual, verbal, bodily, emotional, behavioral, and conceptual information.

In plausible but unprovable ways, a person's life is fictional: serial stories of self, told or kept secret. The stories can hinge on a new acquaintance or viewpoint, a wished-for trait or circumstance, a recurring or fresh speculation, a conflation of events, on mistaken or quasi-true or correct recollections, and other loose but functional hinges on doors that open to self-presentation, inwardly or overtly. I admit to being an unreliable narrator of stories I believe are authentic if not exactly accurate. Realistic fictions? Mythified memoirs? Autofictions? Fallacious nonfictions? I will and I won't apologize for flogging a tired notion to a standstill.

That's that. No more trying to locate and describe an impetus for what I do and its progress to a result, if there is one. All these years of putting words on paper or screen and I still can't answer the question of how that work works. I know the everyday specifics of it, the routine when and where, the necessarily solitary who, the compelling why. The how of it happens, or it doesn't. Either way, it will remain a mystery to me, possibly inexplicable, as baffling as how some memories sink and others swim. Even submerged, they are there, in life's deep waters.

The Reservoir isn't so deep and it isn't always full but there is dynamic life on, in, above, around, and connected to it, a tiny bit of it mine. I explore my small part, question it, reveal or hide it, mispicture it maybe, find surprises, dilemmas, understanding, regrets, and more in materializing some of the waterscape's suggestions.

Or I can and do ignore its appeal when I want to look at larger concerns and tomorrows: mine, my family's, friends', our planet's and the people on it, a miniscule fraction of whom have seen that same absorbing water-scape, breathed its air, listened to the calls of its birds, marveled at its allure, snapped and spread its image for their own recollective pleasure and purposes.

Selected Pictures
at an Exhibition

(with thanks to Modest Mussorgsky and Viktor Hartmann)

"THE OLD CASTLE"

 efore she died at the venerable and, in her case, pitiful age of one-hundred-and-three, my mother lived in the apartment I grew up in. As she got older and frailer, I visited more and more often, as though in lockstep with her decline. I was never sure how she saw me when I was there during her last five years. Was I a nurse? A friend from her schooldays in Vienna? A daughter? A prattling incomprehensible stranger? Her mama? A nuisance? All or any of the above? I also saw myself in several incarnations in that apartment: as a child, a pseudo-sophisticated college girl, a preoccupied young mother, a middle-aged time-stingy rookie writer, an attentive senior-citizen daughter. The coexistence of my different selves occurred in a fugal chorus of voices, moods, and tenses, among them the passive, the present, the potential, the obligative, the interrogative, the conditional. I use those terms allusively but I don't know how some of them function because I never learned grammar in school. In those days, if anyone had mentioned parsing sentences, I would have been certain it had something to do with jail time. Even so, the John Dewey philosophy of learning by doing appears to have worked out okay for me in regard to syntax. Alternatively, chalk one up for Chomsky. Either way, inborn or acquired, the structural rules and patterns are there, at the ready and waiting. Waiting.

"TUILERIES"

Swing the Statues

A rowdy version of Statues. We chose a spinner by counting one potato, two potato. The spinner held one hand of a player, whirled her around and around, then let go abruptly. When released, you had to freeze on the spot, become a statue. If you wobbled or changed position or fell, you were out of the game, which continued without you. Motion or stasis, a long-term dilemma in the making, softy, jellygirl.

Jacks

Using one hand, you threw ten jacks onto a bare floor, tossed a small rubber ball into the air, picked up one jack, caught the ball after one bounce, repeated that maneuver until all ten jacks were picked up. You continued by picking up two, three, up to ten jacks in one bounce. The first person to finish tensies said, "Follow my fancy." We played for hours, fancy after fancy, sitting cross-legged on the floor until our knees begged for mercy or we called it a day, a bore, a disappointment, quits.

Mother, May I

The "children" lined up at one end of a yard or behind a line chalked on pavement. The "mother" stood at the other end. If boys were playing, they could be the mother. "Mother, may I take five giant steps? Scissors steps? Umbrella steps?" The mother said yes, or changed the number you asked for, or responded with other steps you could take. Whoever was first to tag and reach the mother became her. No suspense there, for girls anyhow, in an era when the phrase "Mother, may I?" involved more than manners and pastimes.

Shadow Tag

Another kind of tag. The sun had to be shining, casting shadows. Instead of chasing and touch-tagging a player, the "it" had to run after people and merely step on their shadows to eliminate them from the game. This was supposedly less rough than regular tag. Its somber implications of unsubstantiality, however, were and remain unnerving, even in broad daylight.

"CATTLE"

I am looking at a half-eaten bran muffin on a paper napkin on my desk. I see why I don't usually buy bran muffins. A tiny number of crumbs crossed the borders of the square white napkin, most remained buried under the misshapen mound of earth-brown muffin. The Babyn Yar of it rattles me. Why can't a snack be nothing but a snack? When is a door not a door? When it's ajar, is the answer to that riddle. I can shut the door that is ajar now, slam it, turn away from it, but I can't pretend it's not there, opening and closing unpredictably. I go through it or I don't, mood-depending.

I won't step into darkness today. I say so!

"PROMENADE"

I never read Norman Vincent Peale, but I bought into the title of his bestseller many years ago. I was a chunky miserable adolescent when I spotted *The Power of Positive Thinking* in a bookstore window, and I needed a positive outlook in the worst way. The book's title was text enough for me, strong, rhythmic, and auspicious. I practiced confident upbeat thinking for hours at a time, as though it was a yodel to master that would echo to me on a routine basis, the absence of an alp notwithstanding. That notional give-and-take of shouts became a sometime impulse, but not less appealing or effective. I continue to listen for its vibrant reassurance, which braced me then, a bit, and still does.

"THE BALLET OF UNHATCHED CHICKS IN THEIR SHELLS"

Not long ago, relatively speaking, thank-you notes were often called bread-and-butter letters, though it wasn't bread and butter or even jam we thanked for, it was a charm for our bracelets, a *Nancy Drew*, an itchy angora sweater. In later years, we wrote bread-and-butter letters for wedding presents, baby gifts, flowers received, favors done. We did not send cards with preprinted messages. We wrote our own thanks, mushily Hallmarkesque as they usually were.

The appearance of a bread-and-butter letter was important. The message had to sit on a page correctly, centered, straight at the margins. At a young age, we learned to make snap visual judgments that conformed to some higher norm of neatness, epistolary and more general. Signatures were an entirely different matter, calling for eccentricity and invention. You could encircle, underline, disguise, squash or elongate your signature in whatever way you thought was distinguished or show-stopping.

We wrote on paper called "monarch" size, as I later learned; butterfly or sovereign, either referent would have heartened my girlhood self. Our stationery was likely to be a shade of pink for girls, blue for boys. The pinks often clashed with the lipsticks, stolen from our mothers' purses, that we used to S.W.A.K.—seal the envelopes of letters to pen pals, distant friends, and the many chain letters we joined. My mother's lipstick was called Fire and Ice. I passed hours thinking about the differences of sexy fire and frosty ice, not grasping how such opposites could occur simultaneously on one pair of lips. We did not S.W.A.K. our bread-and-butter letters, though we knew that kisses meant more than any words we could write.

I still handwrite thank-you notes, condolence letters, invitations, and I use many of the stock phrases that I learned long ago. Formula writing, like Formula One racing, has some obvious attractions, such as speed and crowd-appeal.

At this moment, I feel like writing a thoroughly atypical but heartfelt letter of gratitude.

Thank you, dear neurons and synapses, old friends, for your gift that arrived earlier today. I am grateful for your spontaneous suggestion of bread-and-butter letters. Thanks for firing, zinging, branching, triggering, whatever it is you do, I appreciate every little bit of it. Please don't quit on me. I look forward to hearing from you soon again. Sealed with the thought of a long warm hug. P.S. Additional thanks for the full bowl of alphabet soup.

"SAMUEL GOLDENBERG AND SCHMUŸULE"

My knee is sore, mottled with bruises that flag a spill I took on an icy crosswalk. l bruise easily. Black-and-blue blooms appear on my skin as a result of comparatively mild bumps, falls, and elbow-first shoves in crowded subways and buses. The murky bruises turn yellow, then fade away. I know they will reappear on other areas of my body but, so far, they are only skin-deep nuisances. So far, so good. A person I cherish heard the worst recently.

My heartache about her grave situation is discountable in the face of her earned anguish. Even so, I just marked my distress with a hard pinch on the soft inner flesh at the top of my left arm, near the spot where her sentinel nodes signaled the spread of an aggressive cancer discovered three weeks ago. She is undergoing surgery now, and I am under the knife with her in some tenuous way, brooding about superficial contusions and fierce internal assaults, sentinel events, sentinel guards, sentinel nodes, sentinel species, the diverse indicators of danger or change or serious disease or extinction or, in computers, the end of a data structure.

"CATACOMBS"

Early today I woke at the sound of a cry that must have come from the city street below my open window but which I heard, distinctly, as the familiar wail of a hungry infant in the adjoining room. I am still chewing on the mystery of how I sped from dawn patrol, rocking and nursing babies in the half-light, to the graveyard shift, going to funerals too often.

That piercing cry also signaled something else, a practice I haven't thought of in decades that was popular when I was in my post-salad years, not junior or senior, just ripe, peachy keen, as we used to say in a cultural epoch that now seems paleoanthropic.

In those dead-and-gone times, many supermarkets, gas stations, and other stores gave shoppers S&H Green Stamps. As a sale was rung up, the cashier gave you a stamp for every ten cents spent on that purchase. Almost every woman I knew, and millions I didn't know, collected Green Stamps, the earliest of several retail loyalty programs, all providing incentives to stimulate shopping, necessary and impulse purchases, similar to today's reward programs and coupons. We pasted the green perforated postage-sized badges of our consumer constancy onto squares in little booklets with a diligence that edged on obsessive. We pored over the rewards available, as shown in the S&H *Ideabook*, a free catalog distributed at checkout counters. The *Ideabook* pictured goods ranging from bicycles to jewelry, household appliances, lawn mowers, furniture, canned foods, electric tools, clothing, and most other things anyone might need or crave. After we filled the twenty-four pages of a booklet, and had a pile of booklets with enough points for what we wanted, we went to a so-called redemption center, its name amplifying the moral uplift of loyalty-program language that frames consumerism with merit, a sense of achievement, and a system of just rewards. I kept the playpen I got at the S&H Redemption Center in Manhattan for decades, until the day our daughter wouldn't use it, categorically insisting that it was unacceptably confining for her son, our first grandchild.

"PROMENADE"

Running an errand on Broadway the other day, I heard a lilting melody. Mid-block, I saw that the music was being made by a clearly destitute flute player with a gray fedora at his feet. His face had the corrugated ruddiness of a rough sleeper, his beard was matted, his clothes were wraiths of their past. I stopped to listen. He played well, as liquidly as a purling brook or a rose-breasted

grosbeak. Hearing his musical offering to more fortunate passersby, my ears burned with shame, civic and
my own. I left twenty dollars in the hat. He didn't stop
playing but glared at me sternly, reproachfully, as if to
say: Don't bother me! I'm in the middle of a difficult passage. I could see that.

"THE GREAT GATE AT KIEV"

At an approximately biennial lunch last week with three
women who were my bunkmates at the summer camp
we attended for seven of our long-ago girlhood years, the
talk immediately, almost involuntarily, was about any
mechanical or organic slowdowns and failures of our
bodily parts and systems since we last met. None of us
ever deferred maintenance of our physical equipment but,
still, damage happens, and accrues. No damage yet apparent in the memories area, to which we turned with relief
after we concluded our deliberately brief medical reports.

We chatted and laughed about past times, the mischief
we made on a regular basis, the itchy green wool one-
piece bathing suits we had to wear but couldn't find, we
routinely swore to our counselors when general swim
was called on the PA, the campfire singsongs deliberately
garbled by mouthfuls of marshmallows, the thrill-
ing threat of danger from the knives we threw to play
mumblety-peg, the raucous open-truck trips to town for
treats we didn't deserve, the beds we frenched, the boxes
of Kotex we hid, the canoes we swamped on purpose, and
more of the misbehavioral same.

As our desserts were served, the conversation shifted to the now: our ailing bunkmates, one on a collision course with finality, the doings of our grandchildren, the work we are or are not still engaged in, the newest quirks of our spouses and adult children, global turmoil, the digital revolution we didn't anticipate and don't particularly appreciate, our recent travel, volunteer, cultural, other activities. I looked at my old friends and thought: We are here, telling our juvenile tales, sharing anecdotal memories, some news and views, having a good time at our get-together, shooting the breeze, rigorously avoiding the harder darker part of our stories: We are nearing our final chapters. And then? Irrelevancy? Oblivion? Nothingness?

That line of thought doesn't make for congenial conversation. So I barred it, at that lunch anyhow. Why blight a reunion and our appetites?

365 New Words
a Year: October

E**ristic** *adj.* pertaining to disputation or controversy.

The word of the day for the first of October on my desk calendar. It is printed in blatant boldface, a provocation I didn't notice before. I never used this kind of calendar until the beginning of this year. I tear off the previous day's page every morning and discard it, glance at the new word and its definition, but I never saw the unusual word as a challenging shove, not even as a milder nudge. There's an idea. Why not take it for a walk?

yette *v.* to concede.

1-800-FEELING was the counseling referral service number advertised on a placard in the 86th Street cross-town bus. Very convenient, a toll-free call for emotions, as easy as phoning for merchandise from a catalogue, express delivery, satisfaction guaranteed or your money back. What would I order? A red blanket of cheerfulness?

A high-intensity confidence lamp? Yeah, yeah, I chided my reflection in the bus window, 1-800-DREAMER. The sky was blue, the color of truth and constancy, of melancholy, moldy cheese, flatted notes, the void. I got off the bus at the next stop and stomped the rest of the way home feeling like a hammer with nothing to nail.

ventifact *n.*   an object that has been grooved and polished by the erosive action of wind-driven sand.

The pages of my address book have so many scratched-out names and phone numbers and addresses that it looks like an army of inky-footed chickens marched across them, saluting marriages, divorces, moves, job changes, shop closures, estrangements, disappearances, deaths. There is a blank-paged address book in my desk drawer. It has been there for many years. From time to time, I think about using it for the current numbers and addresses of the people I still see and talk with. Then I think again. The up-to-date entries might scuttle my past too abruptly, too conclusively, maybe speed up the natural rate of my heat and energy loss. The slower that entropic inevitability goes, the better. I keep the new address book handy as a sort of protective amulet; its clean ivory pages may ensure my safe passage to a still-unmarked future.

interrobang *n.*   a punctuation mark combining a question mark and an exclamation point, indicating a mixture of query and assertion.

I watched a nature show on television about the various sorts of glaciers and how they move, regardless of global warming. Solid ice creeps, grinds, shears, calves bergy bits, constantly deforming itself to maintain a balance between the pressure of accumulated snow and melt-age. There is a lesson in that information, but its personal application could be seriously oppressive.

mumpsimus *n.*   a person who clings obstinately to an exposed error in practice or expression.

An emailed wedding invitation came some months ago, with links to three websites where the couple was registered for gifts. A printed invitation did not follow, although I waited for one so I could respond as I was taught to do, by hand in ink on paper. After three weeks, I wrote a note to the bride-to-be, whose home address I had to get from her aunt as it didn't appear on the e-vite. We could not go to the wedding in Seattle. I sent a gift, but not from their online lists. A thank-you note has yet to arrive. Sometimes I feel like a kettle that has lost its whistle, rusting steadily, corroded by a new disorder: the prolapse of civility.

jauk *v.*   to trifle or toy with.

A skein of honking Canada geese just flew by, interrupt-ing the sky framed by the window next to my desk. They cut through the air in a neat V formation, wings beating in tight symmetry. I once read that the ancient Greeks believed their alphabetic forms were derived from the sight of cranes in flight: long twig-thin legs and necks and beaks bent in sharp angles. This may be apocryphal lore, but it's plausible enough. I can picture letters of the alphabet gliding and soaring on thermals, swooping down to grab meaning the way red-tailed hawks dive for prey. What were the geese sky-writing just now? V for Voyage? For Victory? Vamoosing? Vitality? Odds are, it was V for Vetoing anthropocentric presumptions.

farraginous *adj.*   composed of various things in no fixed order.

I am getting the hang of daily vocabular challenges. Or am I hanging back, as usual? I falter when it comes to taking chances, in life, of thought, in reckless emotional outbursts. Spur-of-the-moment episodic writing is positively daunting. Even so, these random tussles intrigue me. Reason enough to continue with them, pass a little time every morning with the suggestive pulls and counterforces of uncommon words, flipping them onto my own mat of circumstances. Then I turn to less parenthetical work, though no less speculative or arbitrary.

exiguous *adj.*   scanty, meager; inadequate.

The prayer book for the Yom Kippur services I attended last month has an A-to-Z list of atonement-worthy sins. Trafficking with cynics is one of them. I don't often trade with other cynics, but I do some business with my innate and experientially confirmed pessimism. I swap it for irony whenever the switch is feasible. Irony is a better hedge against disappointment. Or so it feels to me. Both are cheap.

patulous *adj.*   spreading widely from a center;
open, gaping.

The hunter's moon was visible last night, reddish, flamboy-
ant, insistent. I looked at it as a matter of course. The riddles
of the universe don't generally seize my attention. Stars and
planets and galaxies winking in the dark skies are remote
realities. Closer mysteries wow me: the amazements of
happenstance, the manna of laughter, the wonders of love
and the imagination, the transformative democracy of pain.

riprap *n.*   large broken stones used to construct
foundations, embankments, walls or jetties.

The single non-golf non-medical adult magazine in the
ophthalmologist's waiting room was a months-old copy
of *People*. Stale gossip or not, I read it until the drops
blurred my vision. I learned more about Hootie & the
Blowfish than I care to know. Eventually, I was taken into
the examining room. "Any difficulties to report since I
saw you last year?" the doctor asked.

"None," I replied, sanitizing the bulletin. My eyes, at
least, are fine. My heart is another story, one I won't tell.
Many years ago, I resolved never to tap my children's or my
marriage's private circuits for narrative voltage. Sticking to
that plan may smack of censorship, but it has proved to be
a win-win situation for all of us in that tiny junction box.

ataraxy *n.*   emotional or mental tranquility.

Strolling in the park, enjoying the autumn light that
scours the eyes until everything visible sparkles, I overheard one white-haired jogger tell another: "I'm talking

about the days when the Perrier 10K was the big thing. Anyone could join the race. We used to get more than a cup of water after the run. There was yogurt, there were bananas, there was a bottle of Perrier. There used to *be* stuff."

Yes, I agreed. There was stuff. There is still a lot of stuff. I don't want stuff. I want the intangible nuts and bolts of being ready for whatever comes next.

apatetic *adj.*   assuming colors or forms for camouflage.

When I had juvenile faith in the truth in advertising, I believed that being a "Breck Girl" was a cinch, a matter of the right shampoo, a good haircut, nice skin, glasses-free eyes, a smile that revealed straight white teeth, and a soft-edged prettiness that invited approaches. I wanted to be at least a semblance of that iconic American girl of the post-World War II era. I used Breck daily, had the same barrettes and velvet hairbands as the Breck girls, my skin was okay, my teeth and eyes good, my smile a decent copy of theirs. Still, being perceived as a Breck girl was not in my cards, as far from likelihood as heaven on earth. I didn't recognize that improbability until I had slogged through the barrens of middle school, when I saw the Breck girl for the mirage she was. She vanished, only to be immediately replaced by stunning women in Maiden-form bras who dreamed of winning an election, being a firefighter, a toreador, a private eye, breaking the bank at Monte Carlo, being and doing anything and everything. Those lingerie ads depicted glamorous worldly goals to aim for, maybe achieve, even without resorting to sexy semi-nudity in public. My mother was a paragon of cosmopolitan glamour, with allure and dazzle to spare, so my hopes in regard to surface attractions were not entirely farfetched, though mainly unfulfilled. Another mirage met the end it deserved, and remains unlamented.

foraminous *adj.*   full of holes.

I came across the phrase "inherent vice" in *The Economist*, and googled it. It is a term used by lawyers, art and archival conservators, and insurance companies. It refers to the essential instability of a thing's components which contribute to its deterioration or wastage. Also known as a hidden defect, or the very nature of material that tends to decay on its own. Memory is not a material thing, but its vice is also inherent, though clearly not hidden for people of a certain age. My age. I want to believe I still have the ability to recall events and names and ideas at will. Wanting is a lousy substitute for having.

opsimath *n.*   a person who begins to learn late in life.

I went to a housewarming party on Central Park West, alone, my husband is birdwatching in Panama. I should have known better; it was the kind of party that predicts itself with "Regrets Only" on the invitation card. E and J spent two weeks at a tennis ranch in Arizona last April, came home determined to shed their French Provincial skin. They asked a gallery in Phoenix to put together a collection of Southwestern Indian artifacts, and had their apartment redecorated suitably, Nouveau Native, I would call it. Something scrunched underfoot as I walked into the hall where E was greeting her guests. I looked down, saw sand on the bare terracotta-tiled floor. "It was the caterer's idea," E said when she hugged me. The living and dining rooms were crammed with standees, only a couple of people braved the low armless couches uphol- stered in pinto pony skin. There were wee cactus plants on the coffee table, rough-sawn planks mounted on the severely distressed adobe-colored walls for the display of Zuni pots and kachina dolls and the like, a Mission dining table of intrusive bulk with eight matching chairs. I got a drink and squeezed through the crowd for a look at the view, almost bumped into a lit-up glass box on a pedestal against the wall between the two windows fronting the park. It was a cage with a snake in it. I didn't stop to check if it was a rattlesnake, for utter authenticity. I left at warp speed.

concinnity *n.*   a close harmony; a blending.

My father died in my girlhood room in the apartment my mother still lives in. I occasionally enter that room when I visit her, just to be me in a mix of tenses, among them the past, the historical present, the future perfect, the past continuous, and the durative. This could be construed as opening the door to trouble, to sorrow, to youthful confusions, but it doesn't feel problematic or disquieting. On the contrary. I like the teamwork of that gathering in there, my prior and immediate and poten- tial selves in cahoots, pulling together, pooling acquired knowledge and reasonable guesses, making common cause against time's everyday constraints.

klister *n.* a sticky wax for use on skis, as for slopes where snow is excessively wet.

Patience and Fortitude are the nicknames of the lions on the front steps of Manhattan's main library, an imposing Beaux-Arts building constructed on the site of an old high-walled reservoir that piped Croton water to the city when it was still mostly undeveloped above 23rd Street. I like to think of Patience and Fortitude having watery cold feet, although their names refute that notion. Shaky or solid footings, they are an inseparable twosome, paired for life and its ups and downs, peace and strife, bitterness and sweetness, plans and compromises, the whole mixed bag of vicissitudes that shape people's characteristic doings and feelings. I have ups and downs galore, a shortage of unflappable calm and courage on meeting them.

cunctation *n.* delay; postponement.

I take trains on the Northeast Corridor to visit my children and grandchildren. I prefer this method of short-haul travel to flying. It takes me where I want to go, and it takes me back in time, a nice fringe benefit. On a train to Boston last Friday, I thought about how specific travel was when trips by rail were customary. We ate in dining cars and smoked in club cars and slept in cunning berths on Pullmans, saw the particulars of towns and landscapes we passed through. Trains and railroad lines had names that resonated with American hustle and the catchy medley of its sectional breadth: Superchief, 20th Century Limited, Hot Shots, Cannonballs, Bangor and

Aroostook, Atchison, Topeka and Santa Fe, Great Northern, Texas and Pacific, New York, New Haven and Hardly
Moving, as some of us who rode that line in our 1950s
college years called it. When the train I was on the other
day pulled into Providence, I suddenly recalled the gist
of a passage from a novel by Thomas Wolfe that I read
in high school and appropriated as a screenplay for my
own little movie.

It is in *Of Time and the River*, on those few pages
where Wolfe describes a trip made by Eugene Gant, his
fictional stand-in, who is headed north to Harvard on
a train barreling across the Virginian countryside that
sleeps and dreams in the moonlight. I didn't bother with
the Latinate coda of that passage, or with the two apoca-
lyptic horsemen, Pale Pity and Lean Death, who galloped
along with the train. Even truncated, it spoke volumes
to me, a born and bred refugee. It was more than a
picturesque train ride by the light of a silvery moon,
less than a hero's journey to enlightenment. It ground-
truthed my airy hopes, pinpointed my raw hungers. I
wanted to eat up the miles on America's earth as the
pounding wheels of Wolfe's train did, closing distances,
eventually get where I longed to arrive: at a spot to take
root in, identify as an abiding inmost home. I was too
young then to appreciate the now, to acknowledge that a
destination is only a stop, one of many stations on a local
line that terminates where I don't want to be just yet. As
for feeling firmly rooted in America, I missed that station, I was napping when the train reached it, dreaming
other dreams.

I got off the Acela on Friday at Back Bay, thinking of trains that carried human freight to death. Where was pity then?

maffick *v.*   to celebrate boisterously.

A senior citizens group was meeting in the big room off the lobby of the 92nd Street Y, where I was buying tickets for a concert. I stood by the open door for a while, listening to an elderly gent tell the group about a prank he played on his father, decades ago, obviously. I figured the seniors were having memory refreshments, snacks and juicy flashbacks. His mischief involved the temporary disappearance of a set of dentures. As he told the tale, he took out his teeth so that his audience would get the full effect of his papa's mumbled angst. Two other members of the group entered into the spirit of his story, unabashedly removed their dentures and clacked them like castanets, prompting mass mirth. I wished for a minute that my teeth were also detachable, nimble and frisky, and then I pictured all the teeth in that room lining up to dance a can-can, clicking up and down, Rockettes-style, in perfect unison.

shandrydan *n.*   a rickety vehicle.

Identity theft is on the rise, a steep upswing, according to news reports. It is hard to even imagine the double-digit slump of a person whose identity is stolen, let alone shanghaied for nefarious purposes wholly foreign to that individual's character. Still, maybe reclaiming an identity could be more than a laborious salvage operation involving legitimate documents and restored personal and financial reputations. It might be an opportunity for the gut-renovation of self-reinvention. Lose a same old personality, find a new improved model. The hitch is the unclear outcomes of untested choices. The being you know could outshine the one you contrive.

williwaw *n.* a sudden violent wind or commotion.

The density of loneliness caught me by surprise last night, as if it were an unfamiliar experience. I was asleep when I woke with a jolt, shaking, sweaty, heart thumping rapidly. I leaped out of bed thinking: panic attack, panic attack, Mayday! Then I reminded myself that I almost never have acute panic attacks. It was being alone that disturbed my sleep; my husband is still away. The solitariness hit me hard, solid as a brick, heavy as a burden. I made a cup of tea, turned on two lamps in the living room, and sat there sipping slowly. The lamps glimmered like fireflies in the black of the uncovered windows. Ephemeral creature company, at least.

conterminous *adj.* having common boundaries or limits.

Yet another friend fell abruptly and critically ill yesterday. This has been a year of family and friends suffering infarcts, metastases, strokes, fibrillations, vision losses, and more of the damaging same, too frequently. Terminal blight has set in, unleafing the tree of people in my life. I know that age is a big factor in the big picture of bodily health, but I was not ready for a sickscape to impinge on my other vistas. I feel like the traveler who came back from the desert and reported on the shattered ruins of

Ozymandias' once-grand monument; this is some of what I saw.

N's ashen face on the white pillow looked like an eraser smudge. She was getting another bone marrow treatment. I had to wear a mask and sterile gown, stand by the door, couldn't even shake her hand, much less give her a hug.

R, who loves gadgets, his desk and pockets loaded with the latest electronic devices, his kitchen a course in advanced appliances, now has the ultimate novelty implanted in his chest, a new heart. He was the one who joked about his new-model pump, desperate to see a future in his still-reversible situation.

The sunlight on the river bounced off the mirror above the sink and beamed right into M's eyes. Being aphasic, he could not ask someone to lower the shade. After some minutes, I noticed the problem, and adjusted the shade. That was all I could do for him. I am not sure which of us felt more inadequate at that precise moment.

Last June, D took two sets off me with her powerful unerring serve, torso arched back, hand high-fiving the sky in her toss. Two sections of that graceful arch have been removed. We walked up and down a long corridor on the surgical ward and I felt nothing instead of a breast when she leaned on me.

I could but won't report more. Four of my people died. It is time to face the arithmetic.

galluptious *adj.* delightful, pleasing.

There were six yellow apples on a willowware plate on the kitchen table. I took them off the plate and ate two for lunch, studied the blue-and-white scene on the dish while I chewed. A footbridge crossed a meandering stream, fishes swam in the ripply water, a woman stood on flower-studded grass, looking toward a man on the bridge, two birds hovered in the sky, a pagoda rose at the foot of distant hills. I pictured myself in the scenery on the plate, taking a lazy dip in the stream, drying off in the soft air, hiking to the pagoda, going inside for a look. Then the doorbell rang, startled me out of my reverie. It was a delivery man with my dry-cleaned coat. I put it away, went back to the kitchen and quartered the second apple. Once a week I quasi-diet, eat fruit for lunch. I chew each mouthful exactly twenty-five times, I read somewhere that helps to satisfy the appetite. There is also satisfaction in the discipline of methodical routines, some anyhow. Not much. Twenty-three, twenty-four, twenty-five, I swallow.

catawampus *adj.*   askew, awry; on a diagonal.

Regional writing always appealed to me, Southern and Appalachian especially, novels or memoirs that might begin with such a sentence as: *The day our spotted pig was slaughtered and we lads ran off with its scalded hide and hauled it up the flagpole by the P. O. where it flew pink and raggedy as a pair of Sister's knickers was the day my pa swore a whipping was too fine for me, I needed a dose of the county lockup, which purely cruel medicine I was soon to sample.* Or words to that effect. My childhood terrain and its vernacular were nowhere near so naturally breezy and outspoken. Even so, the patch of flinty silence I heard as a child turned out to be fertile, watered by trickles that seep from cracks in stones. This is not a complaint, merely an observation. I see what I see. I contain what I was. The rest is semantics.

diffluent *adj.* tending to flow off or away.

I killed an hour with the mummies. I start work early in the mornings, knock off around noon. When my afternoons drag heavily, I sometimes drop into a museum for a visual pick-me-up. The Egyptian rooms at the Met are my favorites. Gazing at the souvenirs of ancient desert realms, the preserved bodies swaddled in fine linen, the smirking sphinxes and massive stylized statues and alabaster jars and golden dung beetles, I feel time dilating, getting thin and slack, passing anyhow: no crunch, no punch, no point beyond the duration of its moment.

scoon *v.* to skip across water like a flat stone.

These anecdotal fragments are dots on grids of ifs: possibilities of given words. I bingo or I don't. Either way, it's a little breather before I tackle the taller orders of the day. I could use a lift this mopey dismal morning, some pie-in-the-sky treats.

What if people's faces told their whole stories?

What if feelings were facts?

What if the child was not the mother of the woman?

What if the true was the real?

What if I were a Magic 8 Ball with formulaic answers that fit all questions?

What if I stop floating hypotheticals and get down to the business at hand.

pedetentous *adj.*   proceeding gradually or cautiously.

Big birthdays loom too large on our horizons. We should be freer of numerical rankings by now. Still, those decadal birthdays rise like mountains to be scaled and crossed. Approaching, we size them up, check out our equipment, and resolve to move beyond them as quickly and smoothly as we can.

Some mountains are rounder than others, definitely more climbable. I don't recall reaching ten, but twenty was the Berkshires, the Alleghenies, the Catskills, soft easy contours. Thirty was the Coast Range for me, sunny and green, basking in just being there, oblivious to the fault-lines below. Forty was the Grand Tetons, edgy jabs at an intimidatingly spacious sky. Fifty was the Cascades, thickly forested, rainy, a slippery up and down and over. Sixty was the Rockies, in Alaska, cold peaks pointing to promises I hadn't gotten around to keeping, pointing at the clock. Seventy, which I recently crossed, was not mountains, it was mesas and buttes, rugged outcroppings of regrets.

incuse *v.*   to hammer or stamp in, as a design or figure on a coin.

Danger is the ghost in my machine, a phantom that charges my anxieties, denials, dislikes, wariness, all the impalpable forces at work below the surface realities. The danger is notional but pressing: a chronic awareness of what happened to people like me in the war my parents and I escaped shortly before fleeing was impossible. Over the years, I have tried to defy the specter of danger that haunts me, slam the door in its face, gag its alarming moans, overthrow it, outflank it, banish it, bury it. "A" for effort, but I flunked fighting it, forgetting it. I tremble still, safe and sound, ostensibly anyway.

harpocratic *adj.*   pertaining to silence.

A small still-life painting in the window of an antique shop caught my eye as I was walking on Third Avenue. The discrepancy between the picture's remarkable radiance and its humdrum subject matter was puzzling. I stopped to look at the precisely rendered image of a pair of scuffed misshapen navy-blue men's leather slippers angled in a balletic first position, heels back-to-back, toes pointed outward, parked on a shaggy green bath mat on a glistening white tile floor. What were the painter's latent subjects? The tenacity of the domestic? The elegant posturing of exactitude? The false light of things? The poignancy of wear-and-tear? I continued walking up the avenue, feeling more disappointed with myself than with the painting's poker face, wishing I could stop digging for meaty bones that, in all probability, are not cached there.

faffle *v.*   to stutter or mumble; to luff, as the sail on a boat heading into the wind.

"Intheyearstocome you'll understand," my father used to say, speeding through the first five syllables of that pronouncement so rapidly that I heard and thought of them as a single long word. I supposed intheyearstocome was a stage of growing up I would get to, like puberty, which I hadn't yet reached but knew was ahead of me, according to my grade-school classmates who had older sisters. Intheyearstocome wasn't just yucky blood in underpants or moody fits or petting from first to third base. Intheyearstocome would be a higher greater stage of maturity, the onset of lasting understanding. I waited impatiently for that development to kick in, once and for all. Now I know how wrong my simple figuring was: Once and once and once again and again are momentary integers that don't add up to always, don't even approximate it.

whigmaleerie *n.*   an odd or fanciful device or gimmick; a whimsical idea.

A headline jumped out from the newspaper I put on the kitchen counter to protect it from the chore I was doing: Virtual Reality Blurs Line Between the Artificial and the Genuine. I stopped polishing my loafers and read the article carefully. This could be useful, powerful illusions so strong you could chop wood or logic with them. I thought about taking perceptual leaps into computer-simulated situations where character and experience and riskiness and common sense don't sway behavior. Wearing electronic goggles and gloves I could hang glide over Niagara Falls, build a user-friendly metropolis, stroll on the moon, see trees through a giraffe's eyes, drive the Indy 500. The technology exists, is already cheap enough for popular sale. I wondered what would spark ambitions when and if fully interactive simulations of life are readily available. Yearn to be Baryshnikov or an astronaut or Venus Williams? Pop on some goggles and be them without the struggle of becoming them. Too easy, too ersatz, virtually worthless. It might be a good video game or surgical teaching tool, but it's not for me. I smeared reddish-brown polish on the headline. There. Blotched. Actual. My brand of lifelike.

skookum *adj.*   marked by strength or power; first-rate; splendid.

We were sitting in the balcony, Row B. The hall was packed, the house lights down, the audience hushed, the chorus singing its collective heart out in the closing fugue of Mozart's controversially unfinished "Requiem in D minor." Miraculous, I thought, Mozart or Süssmayr or whoosis, this is sublime music. The soaring voices filled my skin, my spirit, I felt vast and emphatically elated. Very soon, I knew, the drums would announce the final notes of the "Requiem," the applause would explode, the miracle would be over. That's that. Earthbound again, as usual. We filed out of Carnegie Hall with the crowd. Two feet on the ground, one step after another. It must amount to something.

Red Light, Green Light

wenty Questions was initially a popular parlor game. It became a weekly radio quiz program, followed by a television show, and is presently online as an interactive game. Its consecutive versions mirror technology's developments, but its guiding rule is unchanged: Only yes/no answers may be given after the customary first question: Is it animal, vegetable, or mineral? Carefully selected questions can shrink the number of possibilities identifying the mystery subject chosen by the designated answerer. Apparently, many mysteries can be revealed by terse yes/no answers to twenty questions or the game wouldn't be popular, or some mysteries are not so enigmatic.

Animal is my first response today. Human? Alive? Female? American? Famous? Do I know her personally? Me? asks my notional interrogator, winning the game with eight rapid-fire queries. This is not a surprise, considering that she persists, in unhesitating words, in directing attention to the who, what, why, how, where, and when of herself and her work. She is not me in anecdotal camouflage.

She is a dead famous American woman, Gertrude Stein, whose *Everybody's Autobiography* I was reading the other day, looking at anyhow, prompted to take it off my bookshelf by an exhibition I saw of paintings that Stein and her two brothers collected in Paris before and between the wars in Europe. I don't recall reading that book but I may have, its dust jacket is torn.

I began to read Stein's book, but the largely chinkless walls of words on its pages made me pant for more punctuational stop signs, room to breathe in, to be and to see in. If I took density for depth and dug lower and harder, would I find that book to be welcoming? A full account of everybody's commonality? As it was, Stein's prose looked forbidding to me. Until, leafing ahead in the book, I chanced to spot a sentence in the second chapter of that book that began: "You are you because your little dog knows you . . ." a categorical pronouncement that left me, a dogless person, momentarily gasping for identity's essential oxygen. I reshelved the book a few minutes later, but that phrase has lingered on several of my thresholds ever since I saw it.

If there are answers to questions about the allure and accessibility of Stein's writing. I must leave them to other people and, ultimately, to The Great Brain in the Sky.

The Answer Man was another radio program that aired weekly in my pre-television girlhood. It was a fifteen-minute program of responses to all sorts of tough questions sent in by listeners. The man with all the answers was Mr. Albert Mitchell who, as I recall, was addressed by the questioner as Albert. He seemed to be answering the questions spontaneously, a flowing fountain of knowledge who, it was disclosed years later, was reading from a script prepared by his staff of researchers in an office conveniently across the street from the New York Public Library's main building on Fifth Avenue. Most people, myself included, who heard the popular program before its fakery was news, believed that Albert was the real McCoy in the brains department, and with total recall as icing on his awe-inspiring cake. The producers and sponsors of the program must have considered the hoax benign enough, and educational for listeners, so a widely broadcast deception entered millions of homes and heads for almost twenty years.

I don't know how many people, if any, who had listened to that program were angry, amused, or even bothered when the fraud was exposed. Did the public's apparent acceptance of or indifference to a patently dishonest practice green-light the advertising and entertainment businesses' increasing flippancy about factual truth?

I wouldn't like to know that *Quiz Kids* was rigged, another radio program I listened to in that era, along with *Information Please*. The *Twenty-One* television quiz show of the mid-1950s imploded in a newsworthy scandal when a resentful eliminated fellow-contestant denounced the scam, destroying Charles Van Doren's brilliant academic reputation, his media-driven stardom, and led to a

Congressional investigation that resulted in the canceling of several other crooked television game shows.

Do today's so-called reality shows have even one authentic bone in their chat-padded bodies? Are televised dancing, cooking, modeling, singing, wrestling, dating, and dieting competitions on the up-and-up? Questions I probably shouldn't ask, as answers won't be given. All the same, I have to wonder about the long-term effects of phonies passing for the real thing.

In a tangential vein, I question the games my grandchildren play. I watch their nimble thumbs darting across the tiny keypads of their phones with tiny screens on which they see and solitarily play a variety of pre-programmed games, or engaging with television sets to manipulate video games by means of handheld joysticks. I want to say: If you think this is playing, you have another think coming. I don't say that aloud, I might get what one of them calls a "hairy eyeball." I translate that as a whammy of mildly exasperated impatience.

At his age, thirteen, I was more than mildly impatient and disgruntled. I squirmed under the heavy itchy blanket of propriety that was presented to me as though it was a precious tapestry to preserve. I threw raucous fits about my parents being Old World fossils, and feared I might be a dinosaur in the making. I chafed, griped, and stewed in my rush to grow up and inhabit my future.

Now, in full Jurassic mode, living in a new technological era, I can see that dexterity of thumbs and narrowly focused concentration are features of virtual play, and my grandkids tell me that warp-speed decision-making is a big personal plus. And maybe it's not, I don't say, sparing them the dinosaur's reflections on the way things were when I was their age, playing games like pick-up sticks, ringolevio, red light, green light, mumblety-peg, hopscotch. These games require a variety of bodily, cognitive, and social skills, such as large and small motor coordination, balance, flexibility, speed, team and personal plan-making, concentration, stealth, self-control, judgment.

I am certain that my grandchildren would enjoy mumblety-peg, but their parents forbid playing with knives, as mine did. I never told my parents that I played with a borrowed single-bladed lethal-looking scout knife daily in my summers at camp during the free period between supper and evening activities. I haven't played mumblety-peg since then, as a parent I also outlawed playing with knives. I can't recall how we scored the game, but I clearly envision pairs of girls in uniform beige camp shirts and dark green shorts, sitting cross-legged on the grass in front of the rec hall, ignoring the fading light and the hungry mosquitoes, throwing knives as if we were preparing for careers in a circus sideshow or training for hand-to-hand combat in close quarters; mind-to-mind infighting wasn't yet on our practice schedules. I also can't recall if the different throws we did had names, but I know that my hands can still position, aim, and release a knife from the ledge of four clenched fingers, or pinch the tip of a sharp blade between thumb and index finger and flip the knife so it loops-the-loop before its point hits and sticks upright in the earth.

Will my grandchildren's thumbs have muscle memories that spark personal and cultural flashbacks? Can mechanistically programmed games provide unpredictable moments of self-discovery? Of actual and dynamic social interaction? Is play a conceptual fishing expedition? A whimsical flight simulator of ambition?

An excess of questions, a dearth of answers, from me at any rate. I could play at being an answer woman, but that sham would be instantly exposed as I don't have prepared responses. Nor do I have the reality or even an illusion of possessing extensive knowledge retrievable at will. I have my share of visual, bodily, verbal, emotional, and situational lore, but I lump that under narrowly personal data, nothing like the industrial-strength recall of far-ranging information that Albert pretended to possess.

Several years ago I happened to talk with a bona fide source of knowledge, a deservedly esteemed art historian. I was curious about the breadth of her learning, and she was generous in responding. She told me her expertise was deep but strictly specialistic, she never aspired to wide erudition. Moreover, even when younger, she was noticeably and distressingly forgetful, which undermined her university teaching career and her appeal as a scholarly panelist. She said her memory no longer bore thinking about, at her advanced age it had as many holes as an abandoned beehive.

Shifting to plain and basic inquiry: Is you is or is you ain't? That truncated refrain of a jazz standard I heard a long time ago has always been a big question for me. It comes and goes through my mind like the subplot of a mystery novel I haven't finished reading, despite having been at it since late adolescence. That recurring theme has several riffs and variations: Is you is or is you what you was? Is you is or is you an idea of you? Both? Is you a shifting cast of yous? Would your near and dear know which you is the you they know? Would your little dog know your different yous? Would you?

Asking questions can be useful. It may be that answers to some of mine are lurking in the deeps of my gray matter, but finding, describing, and conveying them is a far cry from merely housing them.

Sometimes I feel like a carrier of germy uncertainty, a Typhoid Mary who ought to be quarantined before I spread confusion.

If answers to my questions could surface on their own, brisk and definitive, I would celebrate, parade an iconic figure through the streets the way statues of saints are presented to crowds of onlookers on red-letter days. My saint would be the guardian angel of simple constant clarity.

As it is, I have to search and dig for explanations. I should pull up my socks, stop zigzagging evasively and get on with finding some answers before an end game moves my brain into holey's waiting room.

Dreaming of Place

I visited my aged mother several times a week until her death canceled that possibility. Widowed, she continued to live in the apartment I grew up in; I moved across Central Park when I married. The park is half a mile wide, roughly ten city blocks. I did not go far from home, according to the numbers. Numbers are symbols, not real entities or accurate measures of, say, the various distances covered by a person traveling at mutable speeds in several directions over a specific period of time. I went farther than the figures suggest. Still, the lengths I reached seemed negligible in that apartment. Or so it felt when I was there.

Improvements were made over the decades that my mother lived in her Manhattan home, but they were barely noticeable in the living room, dining room, hall, and her bedroom. Apart from new large windows, an expanding universe of up-to-date family snapshots displayed on top of the piano, bookcases, and side tables, and a timely aura of brittleness, those rooms looked as they did in my childhood. Cocoa-brown velvet upholstery and Chinese rugs were replaced as needed with their doubles or close matches. The Art Decoish mahogany furniture, bought in Paris when my parents honeymooned there in 1933 was built to last, and it did. There were fresh but the same pink roses on the table in the hall, books dusted and reshelved next to the books they abutted half a century ago, paintings and lamps in their customary spots. The colors of the walls did not change, nor did the floor wax and cooking smells, the telephone number, china and flatware, the key to the front door. Despite the absence of my father and of the din formerly produced by four boisterous children in the household, it all seemed to be what it was, a place in which I was a little girl, a sullen adolescent lording it over younger siblings, a college student, single and childless, a beginner.

I haven't been any of the above for a long time. And yet, in those rooms where the past and present were intricately knotted, I was a grandmother and a girl in one breath. That simultaneity felt strange, but it must be ordinary. Vast numbers of people routinely visit their childhood homes to see parents who still live in them; some move the ghosts of rooms past into their new dwellings; others live in houses they inherited; still others deliberately recreate a known familial milieu or decorate ethno-nostalgically. For all its commonality, that synchronous feeling was odd. It clung to me like static electricity I couldn't brush off immediately. Ten minutes or so after I left my mother's apartment, the atmospheric charge dispersed and my younger self flip-flopped to present-day realities. Until the next visit. My regular temporal gymnastics should have been good exercise for maintaining flexibility, balance, and a muscular outlook, but it was also debilitating, somehow undermining the solidity of the terrain I slogged or tip-toed or sprinted across during the many years since I left my childhood home.

My mother's living room overlooked the Reservoir in Central Park, a picturesque man-made lake constructed between 1858 and 1862. It reportedly holds a billion gal-lons of water, then estimated to be a sixty-day supply for residents of Manhattan. It was officially decommissioned in 1993 because the city's water now comes from upstate reservoirs. Even so, the old Lake Mannahatta, as it was originally called, is still there, still impressive, as engaging scenery, engineering feat, a haven for waterfowl, and an historic artifact evoking a bygone era in the life of the city.

I often gazed at other historic artifacts with my mother: albums and boxes of old family photographs. Although those snapshots intensified my edgy sense of being junior and senior concurrently, we did it anyhow, to pass an hour, to jog her memory, and it beat the pre-dictable tedium of making conversation that was usually repeated several times. Mountains were always my moth-er's preferred landscape, and there were many snapshots of her enjoying a panorama of alpine peaks, a hike, the crisp air, the sight of bell-collared cows in upland mead-ows thick with summer's wildflowers. One of the photos was a sepia-toned image of her in St. Moritz, carrying skis on her left shoulder, wearing jodhpurs and a Tyrolean-patterned cardigan with silvery buttons glinting in the day's bright sun. She once asked me why that pretty young woman had let herself go, her hips were so big and droopy. That same afternoon, we happened to come across a photo of me in jodhpurs and a hacking jacket on the boardwalk in Atlantic City, nicely but overly dressed for the spavined nags rented at the Steel Pier for half-hour beach rides. I must have been ten or eleven. She didn't recognize me either, in that photo. "The girl needs a haircut," she said. She was right, I did need one.

A hairdresser came to my mother's apartment once a week to wash and style her hair. She was pickled in vanity's brine, not sour but tangy, piquant. Good taste was always her organizing principle. She lost many people, many memories, a sizable number of interesting activities that she relished outside of her home, but she did not lose her soigné refinement or her well-polished social skills. Her clothing, like her furniture, was made to last. She continued to wear some of it, skirts, sweaters, and shoes suitably coordinated: the fast-fading picture of an abidingly elegant woman. When I arrived for a visit wearing jeans or a skirt that revealed bare legs, she never failed to notice and comment on my unflatteringly neglected appearance. I didn't take offense as she didn't intend any, it is just how she received and reflexively transmitted the signals of feminine seemliness.

My mother was elderly when I came to grips with senior citizenship. At that point in our lives, we shared a demographic niche, and many of our categorical designations and personal facts overlapped, but our maps of our worlds were far from identical. Her true north was European, for one difference; mine is the anywhere of otherness. Her residential geography changed several times, but she stuck to her cultural compass, acquired in Vienna in her formative years.

She was born in a village near Cracow, moved to Vienna as a toddler, lived briefly in Holland as a young child, then returned to Vienna. She was Viennese to the core, though she left that city when she married my Belgian father, several years before the Anschluss and what followed it. My parents lived at first in Singapore for four years, my father had a business there. They went back to Europe in 1937 and lived in Antwerp before emigrating to America late in 1938. She told me, more than once, that the angst she suffered about leaving Europe and living in America was eased by her longing to escape Antwerp, a city she bad-mouthed for its steadily rainy weather, its clannish imperatives, and its unmitigated provincialism.

My mother's life after Vienna appears to have paled in comparison to her years in that intellectually and artistically sophisticated city. Singapore, Antwerp, even New York, were flavorless crumbs on Vienna's splendid and satisfying banquet table. That is what she firmly believed, and frequently stated in words to that effect. It is also the gist of a song she hummed constantly, unconsciously

I believed, after she entered her nineties, a song called "*Wien, du Stadt meiner Träume*," city of my dreams, with the refrain: "*Wien, Wien, nur du allein*," only you, Vienna.

I knew my mother's unshakeable opinion about the city she grew up in, I always knew it and tried to devalue it, factoring in the odious and blatant anti-Semitism there, the political and economic unrest, the frivolity of schmaltz and schlag, the narcissistic rhetoric of the intelligentsia, the gaudy melodramatic scandals, the deplorable plague of suicides, and other similarly objectionable aspects of interwar Vienna. My mother acknowledged those negative features, but firmly believed that they couldn't and didn't outweigh the powerful allure of that city. I have to give her credit for maintaining her belief through thick and thin, across oceans, in whole new orders of things and thought. The tenacity of her viewpoint was impressive, as there as the Reservoir, as evocative. Spotty as her memory was, her body mostly housebound in Manhattan, she still dwelled in and on her past in the long-lost context of well-to-do Jewish life in Vienna between the wars. If I felt like a girl in my mother's apartment, so did she, but the place that impelled her throwback was nothing like the one we sat in together.

My mother's home in Vienna was in the Palais Dumba, Parkring, 4. The house is still standing, but I have choices in the matter of travel, so I don't go to Germany or Austria. Why would I vacation in countries where I risk hearing the echoes of jackboots on the march, seeing the afterimage of swastikas on flags? A visit to terror and grief is not my idea of a holiday trip. In the event, I know the family lore about life in the Palais Dumba and in Vienna because its narrators survived to pass it down, and they did, frequently.

My grandparents and their four children lived in a large rambling apartment on the second floor, reached by a stairway in a marble entrance hall. The spacious reception rooms had tall windows fronting the Stadtpark across the boulevard. My grandparents' bedroom also faced the park, the children's sleeping arrangements were less airy and attractive. My mother's room was tiny, separated from the storage room by a green velvet curtain on a sagging rod. Homework was done in the small sitting room next to the dining room. The telephone had its own closet in the foyer of the apartment. The salon was furnished in 18th century French style, and had a piano that my mother and her older sister practiced on, a Bösendor-fer. The boys in the family were woefully tin-eared and never given music lessons, though one of them insisted on teaching himself to play the violin, producing screaks and sour notes that set teeth on edge and sent my grand-mother's little Pomeranian running for cover under the nearest bed. My grandfather, a private banker, had a home office he seldom used but that was strictly off-limits to everyone but the *Putzfrau*. Carp and pike could be seen swimming in a bathtub on Thursday nights, prior to their being cooked by Erna for the Sabbath meal on Friday. Despite some of these homey details, the apartment was, indisputably, in a palace.

When I was a child and a sworn believer in the gospel truth of fairy tales, I took it for granted that the Palais Dumba was what its name announced: a palace, a house for noble people. What's more, I was told that *Graf* Dumba and his family occupied the apartment on the *Nobelstock*, a real Count on the first floor of his own palace. Some years later, I learned that many apartment buildings on or near the Ringstrasse in Vienna's First District were called palaces, in homage to the city's imperial glory days. The street-level floors had commercial tenants, shops, offices, cafés; the upper floors were rental apartments for people of various religions and incomes, the higher the floor, the lower the rent. Jews weren't yet ghettoized or unjustly displaced. Despite my current knowledge about those apartment houses, I still can't entirely dismiss my juvenile notion of my mother, perhaps because it was refueled every time I visited her, or because it mirrors how she persisted in seeing herself: a beautiful infanta in a stately home in a thoroughly enthralling city, her manners as impeccable as her taste, forced to live in exile on rude raw Yankee shores.

She believed she had a special mission in America: to enlighten any philistines she might meet, though such encounters were unlikely in the circles she moved in. Civilizing the natives, she called it. She quit that self-assigned job a few years after undertaking it, turned instead to Europeanizing her children as best she could, pretty well, as it happened, for two of us. The other two are mainly American, in style, in substance, in perspective. My quasi-Continental sister is a historian whose field is medieval

France. I have no such blanket excuse for brooding on the past in another country. What I have is a bedrock warp.

August Ferdinand Möbius, a nineteenth-century mathematician and astronomer in Leipzig, gave a lecture at the Académie Française about geometrical transformations in space, during which he demonstrated the properties of something we know today as a Möbius strip. He took one end of a narrow rectangular piece of paper, turned it 180 degrees on its longitudinal axis, then fastened it, still twisted, to its other end, thereby creating a continuous one-sided surface. He called his new science topology. I call a Möbius strip a model of myself, not demonstrating a transformational truth but describing an impalpable consequence of the war against Jews like me. Time and again, I feel my attention being abruptly turned away from the now in front of my eyes and faced head on with a then I didn't personally experience, can't fathom except by sketchy and fearful conjecture, can't disown or ignore, though I wish after all these years I could loosen its continuing grip on what passes for my soul. So much for wishful thinking.

My mother thought wishfully, idealizing the lost city of her youthful years, believing that it still existed in the reality of her presence on earth. At her advanced age, of course she thought and occasionally talked about dying, but I believe she expected her particular and irresistible Vienna to live on in the tales she told me, in the example she set, in my own lore to pass down. I guess she was right about that, or I wouldn't be putting these particular words on paper.

I don't have my mother's innate elegance and sociability, but I do have her brown eyes, wispy hair, thin wrists and ankles, sharp tongue, a tiny measure of her ample capacity for decorum, something she called her *Sitzfleisch*, a handy trait for the work I do, and her bent for legendizing, another useful hand-me-down from my mother's internal wardrobe.

I am not wearing it now, about to picture her life before I was part of it. This capsule account of my mother's younger years is grounded in hearsay that is supported by photographs and newspaper clippings. The source of the hearsay was not altogether reliable, and it wouldn't be admissible evidence in a court of law, but it is information.

My mother before me.

She holds her nose in the bathroom where fishes swim in the tub, undoes her braids as she walks to school and rebraids her hair on the way home, shudders at the sight of the purplish mole on Erna's goiter when she goes to the kitchen to get her afternoon *Jause* of bread and jam, which she eats at the Biedermeier desk in the sitting room while she struggles with her arithmetic homework. She winds up the metronome before attacking Czerny exercises until supper is ready, sits still at the table, bored stiff, while her papa pontificates about the chaotic state of the economy, goes to bed soon after the meal, sleeps soundly under the eiderdown duvet that previously warmed her *oma* in Poland until she died. Every once in a while, her mother takes her to Demel's or Sacher's on school holidays, where she sips *Himbeersaft* and studies intently, purposefully, the fashionable ladies who gather there like dainty hummingbirds and plump bumblebees seeking gossipy nectar.

In her Gymnasium years, she hikes in the Wienerwald with her classmates on Thursday afternoons, a mandatory outing, boys and girls together, the modern youth. She excels in Latin and history, joins a Jewish swimming club and competes in breaststroke races, murders Chopin ballades, snoozes during Saturday services at *shul*, steals tiny pots of her big sister's hidden forbidden rouge to dab on her lips whenever she leaves the house by herself. She and her brothers take the crack-of-dawn train to Semmering on Sundays in winter, where she skis like the wind until the light fails or it is time to catch the last train back to Vienna. She sneaks afterschool visits to the Prater with her best friends, Lily and Zina, where they feast on unkosher sausages and ride the Ferris wheel, screaming with pleasure as it lifts them high in the sky, their stomachs churning with *Wurst* and daring.

Older, she dresses up for eighteen-button white-kid gloves nights at the opera. *Carmen*, *Figaro*, and *Butterfly* are her favorites. She masters the language of flirtation, slowly but surely expresses her paternal gene for glamour, pledges allegiance to the unflagging and nonpareil charms of Vienna. She nods and smiles sagely at Karl Kraus, Alma Mahler Gropius not-yet-officially Werfel, Freud, Zweig, other local luminaries she passes on the streets, and generally gets smiles in return. She buys notebooks and fountain pens for the lectures in philology at the University that she attends for two years before the *numerus clausus* ousts her. She meets Zina and Lily in cafés known for their literary regulars, where they dawdle for hours in the hope of attracting budding poets endowed with the plus of handsomeness. She pooh-poohs even the idea of eligible young men proposed to my grandfather by a *schatchen*. Vacationing with her parents, she takes the waters and cures she doesn't need at Bad this-or-that and, one fine mid-August morning, literally stumbles onto my father on the esplanade in Marienbad, sending both of the water-filled glasses they were carrying as they strolled, a standard practice at spas, crashing to the ground, momentarily drowning out the music of the orchestra on the bandstand in the Kurpark. As she quickly discovers, he is eligible in every respect, the answer to her papa's prayers and to her own romantic musings.

Twenty-one hectic and exhilarating weeks later, she is nausea-green from the smells of Port Said, en route through the Suez Canal to the Indian Ocean and Singapore, where my parents' arrival is greeted by a squib in *The Straits Times*. She wears billowy white silk slacks and a tight white linen mannish shirt with rolled-up sleeves, the last word in chic, for drinks on the terrace of the Tanglin Club or at Raffles Hotel. At home in the bungalow on Claymore Hill, she won't let her amah do the jobs that the young woman is paid for and ready to do, such as dressing her, brushing her hair, massaging her feet that swell in the humidity to which she will never be acclimated. She tries to teach the Chinese cook how to make goulash and spaetzle, an attempt that proves to be beyond her still-unused domestic talents and the cook's smattering of English. She whiles away her lonely days somehow, reading, writing letters to her parents, sister, and friends in Vienna, plays tennis twice a week at the club with a kill-joy instructor who carps about every shot she makes or misses, takes brisk long walks around the neighborhood, stares into space while the gramophone emits a tinny version of the music she is used to hearing in concert halls, goes to fittings for clothes sewn by a tailor who makes good copies of outfits she shows him in magazines. She perfects her English and French with a retired British schoolmistress who comes to the bungalow two afternoons a week armed with canonic novels by Trollope, Austen, Hardy, Balzac, Hugo, Flaubert, and other such worthies. She waits and waits for my father to return from his office, his bridge game, his stag business dinners, his regional sales trips. She is so consumingly homesick that she feels like a genuine invalid, weak as the flimsy gauze mosquito net draped above the bed, isn't surprised when she has a miscarriage, which she doesn't attribute to the mild case of dengue fever she contracted soon after landing in Singapore, my father's explanation for that failed pregnancy. She has trouble conceiving again, it takes three years. My parents return to Europe when she is eleven weeks and solidly pregnant. Her inveterate seasickness is compounded with daylong morning sickness, and she spends most of the voyage in the stateroom with its convenient toilet, ignoring my father's and the cabin steward's advice about the benefits of fresh air on the decks of the ship, smiles wanly when the steward brings her clear soups, toasted cheese sandwiches, and custards she can't keep down.

She is happy to be back in Europe, though Antwerp leaves her colder than the rain that falls on it incessantly, it seems. The skies are as heavy as her distending belly, but never mind, this baby is kicking and turning as it should, not lifeless like the last one. What she does mind is her mother-in-law's surveillance of almost everything; that woman has eyes that can see around corners, ears that pick up distant rumors, a mouth that spawns behavioral directives like fish eggs, thousands at a time. She can't step out of the apartment on Van Eycklei for a walk or buy a bunch of flowers or meet her husband for lunch near his office on Pelikaanstraat or keep an appointment with the obstetrician without subsequent commentary from her mother-in-law. She begins to see the appeal of the privacy she had in Singapore, disregarding that it wore the label of loneliness there.

When she is eight months pregnant, her mother comes from Vienna to stay until the baby arrives. They buy furniture for the nursery, a layette, a pram, line up a wet nurse, chatter in German, enjoy the novel experience of spending absorbing hours together. Finally, she goes into labor, and adamantly insists on having the baby at home, on the kitchen table, as she always planned but kept to herself until the moment came. She believes that the quality of care in Antwerp's hospitals is dangerously inferior to Vienna's famously excellent medicine; that a kitchen table might be dangerously unsanitary does not dissuade her. Nor can her prudent husband, her frantic mother, or the hastily summoned obstetrician talk her out of her headstrong plan, potentially harmful and clearly unsensible as it is. She gives birth twelve hours later. Which is when and where I enter the story she told to the lilting tune of "*Wien, Wien, nur du allein.*"

In college, I took a philosophy course in logic, hoping it would disable some of the impractical sentimentality my mother generated in me and retrofit me with a plainer cooler approach to understanding life and its challenges. I must have misunderstood the course description in the catalogue because that was truly a false hope, as I learned early in the first of two yawn-inducing semesters of fossilized syllogisms. We studied the traditional laws of logical thought, about which I remember nothing but their names: the law of identity, the law of contradiction, the law of the excluded middle. Ever since I learned the names of those three laws, I sensed that they conjointly described and governed my being and thinking. I can't support the validity of that statement, I can only say that I always felt like a monkey in the middle, running back and forth, never snagging the pink spaldeen being thrown by players on opposite sides. Catching it would make me a thrower, land me on one side, temporarily maybe but there, grounded. This to-and-fro shuttling isn't the same as the passing strangeness I felt flipping between young and old when I visited my mother, or what I continue to feel about the lasting effects of circling on the no-exit Möbius strip of my given history, but it is related to those other states of imperceptible motion. They are kin in my nagging and unreasonable sense of being in transit, a person who doesn't belong where I am, wherever I am.

My mother knew where she belonged. I envy her lifelong certainty of home, of being rooted in a specific place, never questioning her presence there, never loosening the strong bonds of her heart and mind and that place, though she knew her Vienna was gone, a victim of its own vile fascist past. I always wished, and still do, that I could claim a place on this earth as she did, pledge allegiance to it, come hell or high water, be and feel at home there, no doubts about it, no questions either.

A cousin I talked with on the phone last week happened to mention that she went to Vienna two months ago, on business, and that an N. Dumba lives in Parkring, 4, where our mothers came of age; she was rushing to an appointment nearby but stopped to look at the names next to the doorbells at the front of the building. She changed the subject before I could respond to it, and we small talked about our children and theirs, our husbands, this year's chilly summer in London, where she lives.

There was more than met the ear in my cousin's throwaway mention of the present Dumba's presence in his or her ancestral home, and I heard it. I got the tacit message. Unlike the pink rubber ball, it is something I caught a long time ago. I have tried to swallow it but it gets stuck in my throat. Dislodging it is an ongoing operation.

Coda

Two years after writing the essay above, my husband and I visited Vienna for a few days, a trip made for the purpose of my experiencing a place linked to a pivotal chapter of family lore, or so I persuaded myself. I also felt that going there might be an homage to my mother who until her final week of life hummed the tune of a song about the city she loved.

My earlier fears about going to Austria and Germany were not unfounded, but they didn't overwhelm or preoccupy me as a tourist, one among thousands of non-German-speaking tourists crammed into the center of a small eye-poppingly ornate city. Willfully, evasively, defiantly, disrespectfully, wrongfully—whichever, maybe all and more—I was able to muffle the echo of jackboots, dispel the phantom images of swastikas on flags and public buildings, go along with the pretense that new generations of native Austrians have been politically and morally sanitized, skin-deep anyhow. Every so often, on a quiet uncrowded side street, I sensed the residual presence and weight of lives lost in the Anschluss' brutal aftermath, but I wouldn't let it stop me from taking that street to where we wanted to go.

The Palais Dumba was what I always imagined it would be, from the street and inside: an impressive building with a marble entrance hall and stairway, a bit dilapidated but still elegant. A carpenter working on the renovation of the apartment on the *Nobelstock* let us into the building when I told him my mother used to live there, but I wasn't able to see the second-floor apartment where she grew up, though I rang its front doorbell on two days.

My husband and I followed my mother's footsteps through the city of her dreams, to the site of her now-demolished Gymnasium, the University, the opera house, the Prater, the synagogue, the three coffeehouses she frequented, the Stadtpark. It was there in the park, on the third and last day we spent in Vienna, having lunch at an outdoor café next to a table where a woman, her daughter, and toddler granddaughter were sitting, that I felt a tenuous connection I hadn't yet found to that city. The grandmother picked up the little girl, sat the child on her lap facing her, began jiggling her knees up and down, and sang "*Hoppe, hoppe, Reiter,*" bumpety bump, rider. I suddenly envisioned my mother being dandled and sung to in that area of the park near her home, heard that song she must have sung to me, as I heard her sing it to my children, to my infant grandchildren. I silently modified the traditional ditty's already-frightening words as I listened to the Viennese *oma* singing them. Bump, bump through history, little rider, a painful fall on stones here, a terrifying plunge in a foul swamp there, evil ravens devouring you or not, you get back on the horse and keep going, little rider.

It isn't as simple as a nursery song might suggest, but it can be, was, is still being done.

Interior Arrangements

At the supermarket last week, I took a bottle of Italian red-wine vinegar, the brand I usually buy, off a shelf. As I was putting it in my shopping cart I spotted something moving in the bottle, a dreggy gelatinous mass. Though I never saw anything like it before, I knew at once what it was: a vinegar mother: the fermenting starter stuff of vinegar, ordinarily pasteurized and filtered out of the final product. I was about to give that bottle and its murky contents to the store's manager, but it was intriguing, a curiosity, so I decided to buy it, but not use it. Supposedly, there are health benefits in unfiltered vinegars and ciders; this is not a premise I care to test. I reached for another bottle of the same brand, saw that its liquid was as clear as the glass containing it. The woman at the checkout counter and I were chatting as she scanned both bottles without looking at them.

I put the mother-bearing bottle on a sunny window sill in my kitchen, where it glowed like a polished ruby with a visible flaw, which prompted me to recall that jewelers and people who handle gemstones use the word "inclusion" for a flaw.

As the daughter, granddaughter, sister, niece, and cousin of people in the diamond trade, I overheard talk about inclusions in stones when I visited the office of my family's now-defunct business. Until I was nine or so, I thought inclusions were good to have, marks of real and valuable quality, a mistake prompted by all the discussions about them. A few years later, I understood they were natural defects, some obvious and some hidden to the naked eye, some more consequential than others in regard to a gemstone's potential size, shape, refraction of light, grading, and worth. The squishy blob in that vinegar bottle was also natural, but not an imperfection. It was a fecund source of potential generations of its kind, consequential in that capacity but not in a parental role, title notwithstanding.

After a few days, I emptied the bottle, rinsed it, and threw it out; its blubbery mobile innards were getting to me. I tried not to brood about waning away as I watched the vinegar mother circling the drain of my kitchen sink. I didn't succeed. Everything alive—person, creature, plant—must someday circle a drain in one way or another. Only diamonds, as De Beers would like us to believe, are forever.

Yesterday afternoon, flipping through the pages of an encyclopedia looking for an entry on the Law of Parsimony that my husband, a doctor, recently mentioned in talking about diagnostic dilemmas, I happened to spot a Law of Included Fragments, and stopped to read that entry. It is a law pertaining to geology, used for the relative dating of rocks and any matter, solid or liquid or gaseous, trapped in them. The inner deposit is older than what surrounds it. That is understandable, even obvious, but the rest of the entry was beyond me. I had no trouble understanding the Law of Parsimony: Things are usually connected or develop in a simple way, so complex explanations and interpretations are unnecessary and should be avoided. I already knew this keep-it-simple pronouncement as Strunk & White's near-biblical commandment, a directive I respect but don't faithfully follow. Anyhow, I was glad to stumble on that other law, scientific support for my sense of harboring a durable past I didn't live and breathe.

Between finding a vinegar mother and coming across that geologic information within a few days, the notion of inclusion kept cropping up, signaling for attention: I'm here! Now!

Suggestion received. The words "inclusion" and "inclusiveness" have momentous racial, economic, ethnic, legal, political, moral, and religious impact in these nationally and globally divisive times, but I am looking at smaller matters.

Unknowable forever aside, I see a similarity between human beings and flawed diamonds. We do not bend light or dazzle visibly. We are mostly liquid, not palpably adamantine. Our bodily value is computed on actuarial tables,

not weighed on jewelers' delicate balances. We can't be
marketed as investments for a rainy day or hedges against
inflation. We are not material objects used as recognizable
tokens of affection, generosity, or proudly conspicuous
consumption. The thing that imperfect gemstones and
people have in common is an inclusion. Ours is an innate
mass of varied givens: traits, collective memories, looks,
traditions, gestures, and more. The big difference is: A
diamond's inclusion is readily apparent or can be louped,
and is often cleaved away or reduced to dust by a grinding
wheel, yielding a stone that can be polished to transparent perfection.

Among the many givens in my inclusion is a solid and
historic one that can't be removed, much less cleaved or
ground away, yielding a person to be polished like a jewel,
shoes, manners, furniture, performances, and other things,
few of them transparent. In part, the legacy of that specific
given shaped me, not actually but effectively. Even so, I
learned to detour around that inclusion, a given of lasting
consequence that I can skirt occasionally, when I don't feel
up to evoking it.

"Include me out," we used to say in my middle school
years, a vaguely flippant refusal to join a game, a trip
to the bathroom for cosmetic, gossip, or daredevil cigarette purposes, a club of unpopular girls, an impromptu
subway ride to Times Square or Greenwich Village, desti-
nations frowned on by our parents.

My fossilized given included me out, in some ways,
but in other ways it admitted me to a larger world, a
universe of people destroyed but still present, indelibly

evident. It also enrolled me as a life member of wariness' club, located me in milieus that no longer exist, stretched the borders of my concerns, challenged my misgivings, and eventually gave me a license to drive words on paper freeways and byways. Or I seized that license, still take it.

Vinegar mothers and women also have a similarity, but a transitory one. Like those productive bacterial progenitors, women contain sources of possibilities that may or will not become offspring. That's it for generic resemblance. From the age of so-called maturity women regularly lose their procreative stuff until they don't, at fiftyish, statistically. I suppose vinegar mothers retain their fertility if they don't undergo pasteurization, but I could be mistaken. Another difference is: Vinegar mothers don't nest, as many women and animals do, consciously or not, to prepare a clean warm place for the soon-to-be-born. Some women nest for that monthly loss of potentialities, as I occasionally did, still do, when I have a phantom period and suddenly find myself refolding towels, scouring roasting pans, unnecessarily reorganizing closets. It seems as though a vestigial time clock in my shuttered reproductive factory is still ticking, doing its former job without its prior purpose or schedule.

Life dwindling is what I saw, see again today, as the vinegar mother drained away in my kitchen last week. That vivid image prefigures a period of increasing absences: of people, of strength and stature, possibilities, names and ideas, easy sociability, appetite, time, of breath, at the end. At my age, it is natural to think about loss but it is not fruitful, useful, hopeful, fulfilling, helpful, nothing full about it.

I wonder if the nesting I still do sporadically, getting my usually neat home in ultrashipshape condition, is about setting a stage for my final scene. Am I instinctively arranging the look and comfort of it, freshening the air I won't breathe whenever it happens, making it as pleasant as possible for my surviving family? I can't predict when or where or how that last scene will take place, but why not picture it at home, and prepare for it? Readiness is at least an attempt to manage the future's happenstance.

In the boardwalk penny arcades of my girlhood visits to Rye Playland and Atlantic City, along with the customary pinball, Skee-Ball, and claw machines loaded with candy and small toys, there often was a glass-domed wooden cabinet with the head and upper body of a mechanical doll in it. The fortune-telling doll was costumed as a Gypsy crone, a turbaned swami, or a wizard with a tall pointed hat. You put a dime in the coin slot, the doll's head began to nod and swivel, and after a couple of minutes its fingers plucked a card from a rack and put it into a different slot that opened out of the machine so you could get the card. A prediction of your future! Delivered like a piece of Horn & Hardart's applesauce cake! Wishing on faraway flickering stars didn't trigger a material response, never gave me the satisfaction I got from those arcade automatons. I could reach for my future, grab it, add it to my collection of cards that presented possibilities I liked, tear it up if it didn't appeal to me, get a different future for another dime. I heard about fancier fortune-telling machines that talked but I'm glad I never came across one, I enjoyed having a tangible prediction to trash if I didn't want to consider it. That special satisfaction lapsed by the time I was fifteen, but made a comeback many years later when I began to write and routinely yanked pages I didn't like out of my typewriter's carriage, an immediate and vigorous bodily gesture of rejection that can't be made on today's keyboards. Tapping a finger on a delete or backspace key is not nearly so gratifying. *Sic transit* an opportunity for gloriously decisive panache from my previous *mundi.*

I wish my present personal world, small as it is, weren't so fleeting, so chancy. I wish even the thought of antici-patory stage-setting would work like a charm, presto chango, make me believe I am far from ready to quit tidying, cease ticking, slip out to finality. I wish I could refute the evidence of my draining away in droplets, little diminishments but losses nonetheless, most visible, some deeper. I wish—

Enough pipe dreaming! I need to accept the card handed to me a few years ago, acknowledge it, live with aging's inherent and circumstantial givens: its commonal-ity, personal differences and vulnerabilities, random and foreseeable changes, its inevitability, a bedrock fact that can't be avoided or denied at any age. Even still-under-ground diamonds change as time passes, in geologic epochs, I guess, not in our measure of relatively brief years. Synthetic gemstones are another matter.

"Matter" again. That word pops up frequently, like a tour guide's umbrella directing sightseers through crowds on avenues and plazas. The umbrella of "matter" covers many meanings and topics. Its breadth of usage is intriguing, but I won't visit its semantic side streets and alleyways today, despite my natural bent for digression, a trait that could be linked to an ancestral given of necessarily frequent wandering. I can dodge that digressive leaning, temporarily anyhow. Now is the moment. See you soon "matter," maybe. Anything may happen between now and soon.

Afterimages

here are so-called ghosts captured in some early photographs, blurry diaphanous traces of people or animals or vehicles that happened to move through a place while it was being photographed with the long time exposure required at the dawn of camera technology. The ghosts are real entities visible in the picture, though not its intended subjects. I may be making a mountain out of phantom molehills, but I like to think that those nebulous passing presences in a printed image hint at memory's time-sensitive counterforces: clear and hazy, constant and fickle, important and negligible, there and gone.

My memory is not yet a spectral mirage of what it was, but it has seen better days. Other people's storage and retrieval systems may work like charms, mine are balky, slow-moving. Still, I can and do energize recollection almost instantly with a glance at photos of family, friends, events, scenic views, houses, celebrations, vacations, and more: baggage stowed in printed images, put away, mis-laid perhaps, but not necessarily lost in the passage of years, or in translation. A few of my family photos go back a long way, to a different world in other languages, a precious few.

Doting grandparents and holiday cards aside, I don't see many printed snapshots these days. They are giving way to the fast-growing billions of digital photos and videos that are taken, viewed, uploaded, circulated—"shared," in social media-speak—and stored online. Bit-based tech-nology has many benefits, but one glaring drawback is how quickly virtual realities and practices have overpow-ered the experience and impact of once-ordinary behavior and objects. Newspapers, correspondence, professional journals, telegrams, dictionaries, personal diaries, stu-dents' notebooks and textbooks, and library catalog cards are only a few examples of paper things that were useful, popular, frequently essential in recent times, and are now endangered or already extinct species of informational storage, presentation, and access. I use and appreciate many high-tech conveniences, but the decline and loss of tangible sources of knowledge disquiets me, prints of family snapshots in particular. Despite the obviousness of their potential longevity, it appears that their days are numbered. And then what?

Will the visual information on today's digitized images be recoverable on the future's data-processing devices? Get trashed with defunct formats, photo storage websites, and other digital junk? Be marooned in online sites requiring dead users' unknown and forever-secret passwords? Lack resolution due to a standard transmission process known as lossy compression? Have a virtual afterlife? Go AWOL in clouds?

Or will a girl born many years from now leaf through a photo album and discover that she is the spitting image of great-great-great-grandma Rosa? She will if she is, provided that album gets handed down through the generations. Even if she doesn't resemble Rosa, will she wonder about that young woman with her hair pulled back into a bun skewered by a pencil, its ends visible in the photo, her chin tilted up to showcase a slender neck, wearing a white dress with a striped ribbon accentuating her slim waist, two books tucked into the crook of one elbow, the other hand gripping the top of a painted wooden walking stick? Will that girl want to know her ancestral faces and stories?

Rhetorical questions; unsupportable answers. One probability is that there won't be a revival of meticulously lifelike portraits by painters in any up-to-date art biz.

Over the years, I looked at that photo of Rosa, my maternal grandmother, taken when she turned seventeen, her birthday noted in silvery ink below the picture, the earliest image of her in an album I have. I saw that she was pretty, and ventured to think she was peppy, playful, her confidence tinged by a hint of vanity, her wry smile an unvoiced observation, and champing at the bit to get going with her future, as suggested by the determined frontality of her gaze and stance. Bolstered by family lore, I envisioned some of Rosa's youthful feelings and doings. I saw her foot stomping defiantly, her parents indulging their high-spirited only daughter whose three older brothers also humored her, her mischief an end run around boredom, her yen for more education than girls got in those days, her talk-of-the-shul-sisterhood crush on the cantor's hooligan son, her unseemly impatience with the niceties of needlework, cookery, flower arranging, other domestic arts.

Rosa married two years after that photograph was taken, a fine catch, arranged by a *schatchen*. She gave birth to four children, one every two years, moved from a small town in Poland to big-city Vienna, and appears to have relinquished her willowy shape, her pride, her humor, her daring, it seems, in the handful of photos I have of my mother's parents before the Anschluss. My grandfather, tall, terrifically handsome, successful, authoritarian, overwhelmed Rosa, outshined her, outgrew her, sidetracked her. Even so, in the stiff-upper-lip decorous-little-wifey photos taken in Vienna she seems stronger, sprightlier, than the anxious woebegone woman I saw in New York.

What I didn't know until recently was what broke the remaining vestige of Rosa's spirit. She was unfixably shattered by war and a series of displacements that sent her, alone and without a passport or any other documents, from Vienna to Antwerp to the beach at Dunkirk. She arrived there when over 300,000 British and Allied troops and crowds of unenlisted European fugitives were being evacuated from France by all sorts of military and civilian vessels: a massive throng of people enduring, outliving, or not, the constant *Luftwaffe* bombing of that beach. Rosa pleaded for and got passage across the Channel to what she believed was safety in England, family there anyhow, and turned out to be a prison in London. She was incarcerated as an enemy alien. She didn't speak a word of English, so couldn't explain to the prison authorities who interviewed her, none of whom spoke German, Polish, or Yiddish, that she ran for her life, didn't have time to go to the safe at the bank for her documents, and headed for England because one of her daughters was settled in London, a person who would vouch for her identity and innocence. Her other daughter had recently emigrated to America, but could send any papers or affidavits needed. A rabbi who spoke German visited the prison one morning eight days after Rosa was jailed. He promptly contacted my aunt, and Rosa was released a few days later.

Why she absolutely refused to leave her home in Vienna with my grandfather and their two sons who fled ten weeks before she did, and why my grandfather didn't insist on and prevail, as he usually did, about her going with them, is still a mystery. If Rosa had left Vienna with her husband and sons she would have been interned in a refugee camp in Marseilles, but not alone, maybe not broken.

Rosa came to join my grandfather in New York soon after the war ended. She wasn't "the vaguest trace" of her former self, according to my mother, but I was never told why, and was reluctant to ask. Our family was strictly tight-lipped about the war, especially *devant les enfants*. I knew, vaguely, that Rosa made a solo flight to England, but I didn't know she landed in prison until last year. I was visiting a cousin in London, and she reminisced about her childhood home in Hampstead and the presence of our grandmother in it.

I would have liked to know Rosa better, to hear and understand her songline, the map of her journey through life. Aboriginal Australians of different tribes chant their songlines to each other without language barriers; the melodic line, rhythmic patterns, and traditional order of songs describe the landscape and the paths to take across it, tracks created by ancestral spirits in mythic Dreamtime. I had significant verbal and temporal barriers with Rosa. I knew her for a mere nine years, by sight mainly, as we didn't speak the same languages apart from rudimentary exchanges, such as "*Bitte*, Oma, can I have another bonbon?" and "Gin rummy!"

I still know Rosa by sight.

There are only glimpses of any person or place's story in a photograph, momentary views that are partial and skewed but generally accessible, more or less evocative, inherently questionable, incidentally historical. The notion of seeing a life on small pieces of paper is both intriguing and disconcerting. It seems careless, inadequate, reducing a person's story to paper-thin residues. It also seems full and appropriate: a look at the linear commonality of life's photo opportunities: birth, growing up, mating, rearing the next generation, getting old. Somewhere between the extremes of individual and universal is a reason to look at photographs, to think about the different telling details they frame, the time they stop, the faces and events they distinguish, the questions they ask. Photographers often make choices about the content and mood of photographs they take, but a printed photo stands on its own two feet, speaks for itself, or doesn't; eloquence isn't guaranteed in image-making.

I have always been puzzled about why color photographs look frankly fictitious to me. Given the colorful world we live in, they should look more realistic than black-and-white photos, but they don't, not to me, perhaps because I first saw Kodak color prints when they came in two tones: garish and improbable. Or it might have to do with the way dazzling surfaces eclipse plain-Jane details. Whatever the cause, the effect is the same: I find it hard to trust information conveyed in color photos. As for the digitally manipulated images ubiquitous on all sorts of screens, in museums, magazines, and other visual media, they are by definition untrustworthy, models of inauthenticity. Fortunately, there are plenty of lens-based straightforward images that I can poke around in, maybe see something new in them. That youthful photo of Rosa, for one.

I never saw myself in that picture until the other day. I was dusting books and came across the album with

that photo in it. I unshelved it and took another look at
Rosa, the first since I learned about her wartime ordeal.
I am linked to her by genetic material, some traditional
practices, a few orally transmitted anecdotal tales, some
artifacts handed down by my mother—the usual family
trappings—but I don't resemble Rosa, not in appearance
or temperament, not in life experiences, not in death from
cancer when she was younger than I am now. Although
I saw that photo of Rosa many times in the past, something about it was different when I looked at it last week;
it seemed bleaker, somber. Her forward stare had an icy
flatness, as though she foresaw the loss of her hopes, high
spirits, opportunities, eyes fixed on the vanishing point
of her given world.

What I recognized in that familiar image was the shattered woman Rosa became, a person I knew so inadequately.
I also identified something about myself loading that picture, a forward-thinking hope I nurse like a nest egg.

I may be trespassing on dreamland, but I want a girl or
a woman or several, my female blood relatives in future
eras of brand-new game-changing technologies, to have
and to handle printed photos of me, study them for a
possible likeness, locate them in a cultural moment,
mine them for our mutual or her own paydirt. Here I
am, young and older, warts and all. Take a good look. See
me. Wonder about me. Read my image, at least. One of
these years I will quit this world. I will be buried, and my
words, spoken and written and mostly unpublished, will

disappear like unprinted digital photos, a passing convergence of pixels, airy litter consigned to ethereal space and earthly shortsightedness.

In the meanwhile, I am still present. Age hasn't yet fogged my mind or tampered unduly with my body's clockworks. I have time, time to think about having time, time to waste, to fail, to speculate, to bark up the wrong tree, to worry about the small stuff, little matters and things, such as tangible photos that could last and someday engage and inform attention, turn looking into seeing, grasping, comparing, identifying, reflecting, and more: the big picture of human connection-making captured on little pieces of paper in the language of sight's universal vernacular.

So long as I have time to spare, and my hope doesn't turn cold like Rosa's stare, I will continue to track words across pages, my kind of songline, and to stockpile family photos, put some in albums, store the rest in labeled shoeboxes.

Mollusks and My Worlds

If a person is, as John Masefield wrote, "A thing of watery salt/Held in cohesion by unresting cells,/Which work they know not why, which never halt . . . ," then I would like to tinker with that image by polarizing it, see some people as tidal ponds, bodies of water behind high and stable dunes, their surfaces ruffled by tides flowing through a narrow inlet, and only occasionally roiled by storms. On the opposite side of those dunes are people who churn and whirl recurringly, caught in the uprushes and undertows of their choppy temperaments. Much as I would prefer to be a pond, I know my preference is unrealistic. Which doesn't stop me from taking its what-if bait.

What if I were certifiably unflappable, cool, patient, and in a steady state of tension-resolved balance?

I would probably be a) six feet under; b) someone else; c) an Attic statue of Athena.

Another answer is: I would have the light breezy touch my piano teacher had and preached.

Yet another is: I would be as soft and spreadable as room-temperature butter or Pond's Vanishing Cream.

And what if Pond's had done the magic?

When I was seven or so and gullible to a fault, I hoped a cosmetic called vanishing cream would work. I knew women smeared it on their faces morning and evening, or anyhow my mother did. I wasn't allowed into her room while she did what she called her toilette, but when she emerged I could see that putting cream on her face didn't make her face disappear. Still, I wished it would magically make me vanish for a little while when the time was right, probably in a few years. I absolutely believed that magic could happen. I had watched magicians at birthday parties, and with my own two good eyes saw silver dollars, a hamster, hair ribbons, and charm bracelets disappear in a flash, in a breath, poof, gone! I was glad to see that the magicians brought those things back, they could have left them wherever they were, not there, for sure.

Soon after I turned twelve, I shoplifted a green-lidded glass jar of Pond's Vanishing Cream from the cosmetics counter at Woolworths on Broadway. I felt old enough to disappear, or at least attempt to be gone. Although I no longer believed in hocus-pocus tricks, or that a word's meaning had to predict its effect, I figured that the faint possibility of vanishing cream keeping its promise was worth a good try; I had nothing to lose, nothing spent on the cream either. The next Saturday afternoon when everyone was out of our apartment, I locked myself into the bathroom I shared with my little sisters, undressed, stood on a bath mat and slathered the oily glop onto every inch of my body, face, and scalp. I turned the shower on, only the hot water, to steam up the small space, make clouds of mist to drift away on. I didn't want to disappear permanently, only to leave for a short time, bye-bye, I'm going now.

Of course I went nowhere fast, faster than a hamster or money could zip out of sight.

I don't believe I actually did this. It seems and feels to me like a vision sparked and fleshed out by several recurring and insistent memories with minds of their own, all vying for attention, demanding I give them at least the temporary presence of words on a screen. I began this morning thinking of tidal ponds, recalled my unshakable faith in magic, my mother's routine use of Ponds, shoplifting at Woolworths, my sense, then and still, of my unworthiness in the face of tragedies across the ocean that ended in showers and smoke. What I didn't understand at a young age was that merely being missing, bodily or notionally, even for a second, was a vain, shameful, and deeply offensive way to connect with the millions who vanished. True or false or patently dubious, the vision I likely had and reported above is tethered to questions I couldn't ask then, can't answer now, and can't stop trying.

Here, today, keyboarding words, I need to say that I don't
know how many memories make a whole lot of sense,
or if my connection to that immense absence is close
enough to be a legitimate part of my being. Rightful or
not, immediate or second-hand or at a remove, the connection is there, persistent, an absence that surfaces on
its own when it needs to breathe, see the light of day.
Though I am used to its coming and going, its presence
forces me to envision it, see myself in it, make the connection, as I must have done above, unconsciously, on
memory's automatic pilot mode. It is a sight that always
troubles me. Too bad, tough luck on toast with strawberry
jam, as we said in the days I shoplifted, many years before
sarcasm's motor was reengineered as "ironic" and could
refer to a demographic in Brooklyn or a T-shirt.

A New Yorker since my infancy in Belgium, and a chronic
pedestrian and rider of public transportation, I don't
spend much time in cars, but they have a standard feature
that invariably catches my eye the moment I sit in one.
I see the warning engraved on side-mounted rearview
convex mirrors silently alter one word of that brief cautionary message, and it speaks volumes to me: Memories
in mirror are closer than they appear.

It would be fine to know for a certainty that some
memories could be permanently distant, those selected
for banishment to a remote inaccessible region of the
brain, the ultima Thule of oblivion, but that hasn't been
my experience. I could be a born flop at forgetting. And it's

sure as fate that I was raised to heed and retain the lessons
and lore firmly stitched into my young memory's impressionable fabric, fuzzier at present but still orderly. Perhaps
my inclination to reflect on the past is happenstantial, or
a professional warp, or a dearth of other material. Whatever the cause, the upshot is that I sometimes feel like a
snail inhabiting and hauling a shell of memories, mine
and some others not directly my own, all of them leaving
a thin visible trace of a fleeting passage on earth.

In the American Museum of Natural History, near the
77th Street entrance lobby that was refurbished several years ago, there used to be a small room with the
title of its exhibit on a sign above its entryway: Mollusks and Our World. That room is now a snack bar, that
exhibit was moved to a nearby corridor and demoted to
Mollusks of New York State, a misnomer, as there are
a few mollusk specimens from other areas and continents. Over the decades, I went to see that exhibit many
times, mainly to refresh my ideas about the advantages
of having a hard shell like conchs, whelks, snails, clams,
murexes, and the like, but not always being stuck in it.
Some mollusks, those of the gastropod class, can move
parts of their bodies in and out of their shells, responding
to the presence of enemies or obstacles, the food supply,
the social and procreational opportunities, the nice or
nasty weather. A drawback to being a human mollusk
is not having a vertebral column; being spineless is a
distinct disadvantage in our species of life. The ability to

clam up is a marginally more useful trait. As for being a crab, a worm, a leech—other invertebrate creatures related to mollusks—I choose to deny or ignore any evidence of those labels appearing on me.

The taxonomy of the animal kingdom boggles my unscientific mind. All those phyla! All those classes, orders, families, genuses, species, and all their sub classifications! Long chains of terminology that, Houdini-like, shackle my brain before escaping it. The scientific classifications of the vegetable and mineral kingdoms are equally mystifying to me. If I want to know a little something about a form of life or an inorganic substance, I turn to my helpfully big dictionary for a capsule account of its basic nature and qualities. Or I take a quick online wiki-peek, a source of info lite, info faux also. I skimp on doing more thorough research because I feel pressed for time; senior citizenship generally boosts the frequency of clock-watching and lowers the prospect of absorbing new data in fields of inquiry you never studied after high school.

I regret not knowing more facts, rigorously proven information that might refute many of my hunches and impressions. Too late to feel sorry about not having the benefits of meticulous scientific thinking and some of it findings. I don't usually feel sorry about being late because I routinely arrive early for every appointment, event, plane or train departure, as my father did, as my children do. If I were a bioscientist, I might consider trying to identify a promptitude gene.

Innately prepunctual or not, I am tardy in an important way: slow to arrive at firm decisions, only some of them work-related. Sluggish describes my usual pace on bylanes of ifs, buts, whys, maybes, and similarly rambling paths, some of which lead to clarity and action, others to dense obfuscation. The odds of logic are stacked against unmethodical ruminating, but I take the chance, necessarily and frequently in life, voluntarily on what passes for paper these days. Hours aside, I don't have much to lose in typing easily deletable words that skim across a computer screen like water striders on a pond or, as it happens, like the floater presently skittering on the watery surface of my right eye.

That tiny dark speck came into my life about a year ago, darting around the field of vision in that eye. It isn't bothersome or alarming, it is just there, a presence. Sometimes my floater has company, not visiting specks but saw-toothed flashes of light circling the same field. The pulsing lights disappear after a few minutes, the floater stays, for the time being anyhow. An ocular migraine is what my ophthalmologist called those flashes when I asked about them. I call them my northern lights, only occasionally seen at the latitude I live on, always spectacular, an irresistible view of light waving and shimmying in the sky.

A view can be elevated to a viewshed, also called a zone of visual influence. It refers to an area visible from a specific vantage point, a sight that has natural or historic or

scenic value and merits attention. Protecting and preserving viewsheds can be a contentious issue in the politics of
land use, zoning, and real-estate development. The grand
and mostly pristine sight of the age-old New Jersey Palisades directly across the Hudson River from Fort Tryon
Park in upper Manhattan was the subject of a lawsuit to
stop high-rise building that would alter and spoil the
view, a suit won by the viewshed advocates. Profiteers
may challenge that verdict someday, and it may be over-
turned, but for now the sight is safe.

People have viewsheds that are part of a bigger picture,
one that isn't visible from a scenic pull-off on a highway,
a skyscraper's observation deck, a platform overlooking a
battlefield, a mountaintop, or any place on earth. Human
viewsheds are internal and include both personal and
generational views, and stretch beyond the scope of any
individual's perceptions, widening into a collective zone
of cultural influence. Some of those influences lasted
longer than the statistical thirty years of a generation,
others imploded sooner. Preserving the allure and impact
of my generational viewshed is a mirage about to reach
its vanishing point.

My personal zone of influence was always a bridge,
and my particular vantage point is the middle of that
span: the spot I stand on to see what is there on both
sides, a dual perspective that informs many of my characteristic outlooks.

I used to feel odd but okay with having double vision,
not actual diplopia, but a sense of seeing two things at
the same time. A child of refugees, the two worldviews

I saw simultaneously were prewar Europe and postwar America. My early focal duality remains active, though sometimes subliminally on the job. These days, I also see and connect other worlds, similarly dichotomized. Along with my contemporaries, I span past and present; resilient and brittle; young and old; paper-based and screen-dependent; central and sidetracked; sharp and dulled; slow and speedy; other categorical polarities.

The ups and downs of a life may be unpredictable, but some of the forces they exert can be resisted. Most people in my senior-plus cohort tend to defy the lows, though not always successfully. We don't want to cave yet, surrender to irrelevance accelerated by disuse, indifference, diminishment. The universe may operate on the inescapable eventuality of heat and energy loss, but why not ignore any such depletion until we can't, when and if it hits us like a Mack Truck, flattens us on the road to our exits.

Many people in my generational sympathy group resist the powerful pull of technology when we can, not often these days. If necessary, we move part of our daily doings into the online world, then inch back into our ingrained, maybe fossilized, ways of learning, shopping, socializing, killing time, and more. Our resistance is definitely counterproductive and retrogressive, but it is also understandable, rooted in uneasiness about the growing impersonality and unreality of digitized everything available on demand for instant transmission to distant people, to robotic devices. And that's not even a beta model of what's ahead. From my generation's age-shared standpoint, the future looks like a lonesome state of being. This may echo a tiresomely familiar litany of lost practices and opportunities croaked by old-timers afflicted with toothless dissatisfactions or nostalgia so crippling it verges on lamebrained. Even so, far worse than complaints, comparisons, and tedious repetition about virtual immateriality, there is actual nothingness, vast and unfathomable, inescapable.

Another pull we feel but can't effectively fight or sidestep is loss: of other people, of our own solidity, of time. Aging is more erosive than many of us anticipated, I for one. I must have been blindfolded and terminally wishful to think that less might pass for a credible semblance of the same as before. I had another think coming, and it arrived loud and clear, a plain fact, hard to deny, hard to accommodate. Still, if the simplest of tiny organisms could rise from an ocean's dark depths, then inch up through muddy slime into life-altering sun and air, I should be able to adapt to my changing reality.

Glassworks

Walking past a greengrocer's outdoor display early this morning, I saw a nursery full of preemie vegetables. There were bunches of wee carrots and beets, rows of tiny okra, mini squashes and eggplants, marble-size potatoes, embryonic corn, darling microgreens. It looked to me like infanticide, slaughter of precious little cuties to be offered in the arms of an over-sized plate.

"'Cute' rots the intellect," according to Garfield, a cartoon cat who delivered that pithy statement in the early 1980s. Andy Warhol, a gnomic faux-naïf guru in those days, apparently admired Garfield's quip because those words were stenciled in large red letters above a doorway in the entrance hall of Warhol's final studio, his third so-called Factory. This is secondhand information, a friend's report to me many years ago.

That crisp incisive motto appeals to me also, for its brisk assurance, its lack of mealy-mouthedness, its promise of probable cause and effect, its admirable brevity. It is not taped to the wall in front of my desk, but I did jot it down soon after I heard it, put it in my folder of words, phrases, and ideas stored for future use, perhaps, but mostly verbal bric-a-brac. As it happened, some baby vegetables spoke up for that note today.

I don't believe the powers of my mind have been rotted by cute, time is the likelier culprit. It has meddled with my former ability to swiftly recall names and phone numbers, to handle difficult situations as they unfold, to promptly see my misjudgments, to make plans beyond the upcoming year. As for my work, a relentless ticktock affects abilities that I used to take for granted. Such as foreseeing where a newly started essay might be headed, immediately hearing the passing dissonances of words, recognizing my unforced errors before I get tangled in them. Still, I persist in defying time's petty thievery when I write. I go where the words I happen to be using lead me, or I don't, find other words to follow, risk not locating a path, frequently stop to trash what I am doing, period! This may not be persistence on my part, acceptance of some shortfalls is more like it.

With or without me, my systemic and occupational lapses, my hopes, efforts, and decisions, time will anyhow deliver futures that will stay for a while, then amble into the past. I am here today, a fact to greet with thanks. I am also grateful for today's freely given help from some cunning little vegetables.

I don't generally count on assistance from sources outside of my head, but once in a while it arrives unpredictably. I read for a couple of hours every day, when life's demands happen to be loitering on the outskirts of necessary attention. My reading is more recreational than helpful, but if a word or phrase or notion grabs my attention, I write it down, stow it in the folder mentioned above, seldom use it. Visual experiences are more immediately effective for me than verbal ones, and there is greater personal leeway in what is seen; words have dictionary-decreed meanings, often multiple ones that tumble and twist like gymnasts. Seeing is straightforward, instantaneous, a glimpse of something that may suggest possibilities. Such as today's sidewalk display. Such as what I gazed at three days ago.

I was in Philadelphia, visiting a granddaughter in a college near the city. I went alone, my husband was birding on Cape May that weekend. On my way to the station for a train back to New York, I stopped at the Philadelphia Museum of Art for some visual refreshment. I took yet another look at a complex artwork: Marcel Duchamp's "The Bride Stripped Bare by Her Bachelors, Even," informally called "The Large Glass." It is an important and celebrated work that I do not understand or like, even. I have seen it several times, but never wanted to learn about it because its hushed mystery feels restful to me, a recess from everyday activities and enigmas, human ones mainly, that clamor for explanation, understanding, and, often, acceptance. For ten long minutes I stared at that

puzzling work with its odd mechanical forms, spidery
wires, meandering cracks, dust trapped between its two
panes of glass, and intersecting circles. Baffling as ever, I
was glad to see.

Leaving the museum at its back entrance so I could
take the stairs down to the sculpture garden, I spotted two double sculls that appeared to be racing on the
stretch of the Schuylkill River below the hill on which
the museum is perched. I wondered if the rowers were
women or men, I was too far away to see that detail. I
lost sight of the sculls as I walked down the stairs and,
as if in sensory compensation, a French phrase I seldom
hear rustled in my ear: *l'esprit de l'escalier*, staircase wit, an
expression that refers to people thinking of a smart retort
or remark only when they reach the end of the stairway
leading them away from the site of a dispute or vexing
conversation. Too late, in two words.

Recalling the sight of the sculls has cued an opportunity for me to look at other boats, some I missed, some I
caught, some I still wish to board.

The sleek speedy professional women's powerboat left
the dock without me. Cold comfort to know that only a
tiny fraction of women in my generation boarded that
boat early on, learned to fuel it, handle it, make waves,
dock it skillfully, abandon it if necessary. Most of us who
came of age in the late 1950s were otherwise occupied,
minding our children, our domestic business, our P's
and Q's, persuading ourselves that we didn't mind being

passengers on a slow boat to nowhere new and different. Eventually, an appreciable number of us made something else of ourselves in worlds beyond our familiar harbors. Even so, we were on the late side for reinventing lives, too late for too many women.

Another boat I missed handling is a canoe, preferably an old wooden green-painted one. I would have liked paddling a sturdy time-tested canoe almost noiselessly, deftly, steadily, across any body of water I might encounter in fair weather or the foulest. My liking couldn't translate to actuality: I am not a person inherently suited to quietly feathering her paddles or to steadily riding out heavy storms.

I did ride out a big storm on the ocean liner carrying my parents and me to safety in America. I was an infant, so hearsay is what I know about that voyage. We left Rotterdam one sunny September morning, headed for the port of New York. Our arrival was delayed because the ship was violently and dangerously battered by fierce winds for two days and nights in the sea off Rhode Island during the hurricane of 1938, called The Long Island Express or The Yankee Clipper for the speed of its approach and destructive landfall that were not accurately forecast. This was a few years before hurricanes were given women's first names, as if an informal and friendly designation might lighten their damaging impact; thirty-some years later, men's names were added at the insistence of feminist activists. Damage is damage, greater and lesser, named or not, palpable or intangible. Mine, of a historical nature, crossed the Atlantic with me.

Catboats are appealingly simple. The single sail is easily raised and belayed, the tiller a mere push-pull directional message to the rudder, the centerboard is up or down, the telltale at the top of the mast clearly visible, a bailing pail is at hand. I have sailed catboats occasionally, on vacation in places where boats could be rented by the hour, the day, a week. I always wished my everydays could run with the wind, on a broad reach, the water sparkling, the breeze a gift, simplicity the belaying cleat.

I would have liked to pilot an icebreaker. I could have opened a passage through the layers of frozen arctic snow that chill some social occasions and their attendees. In friendlier situations, I might have made more headway with new acquaintances. The Inuit and Yupik have many different words and compound words for various kinds of snow. I have a few words about my inmost navigational lanes; guarded, indecisive, gutless.

Lightships appeal to me, though I couldn't board one these days apart from those embalmed in maritime museums. There are few lightships still in use, and those are untended, their crews obsoleted by satellite and onshore monitoring of maritime conditions. Anchored in places where it isn't practical to build lighthouses, they provide navigational aid to nearby ships and boats, flashing bright warnings and sounding horns: danger ahead, avoid these rocks, shallows, fogbanks, brewing storms. Strictly speaking, I couldn't be on an unpeopled vessel as my presence would populate it, but at times I feel I am on the deck of a lightship, watching it beam cautionary signals, hearing its shrill horn.

I just got an alert. Get out of the boatyard. Now!

Now is now. It is also won in reverse. Writing is not a race, a card game, a disease cured, an election, but it is a challenge. I can take it, postpone it, walk away from it. Some days, I see that challenge as washing floors without a mop in hand, only a bucketful of soapy slippery ideas. Other days I view it as a duel with my memory, no masks, suited up with layers of former experiences, feinting, lunging, maybe making a touch on something to think about. I often engage in that duel, believing I have at least a sporting chance.

This is definitely TMI, as my grandchildren text. I write or I don't, and that's the all of it: a simple yes/no statement, staircase wit not required.

Earlier on these pages, I revisited an hour I passed at the museum in Philadelphia. That has now led me, with some detours, to looking at my own work in the context of "The Large Glass" and my reconfirmed response to it.

Language is also and frequently baffling, a puzzle I tackle necessarily, carefully. The mysteries of writing are not hushed or restful or a matter of simple transparent decisions because so many words are layered, odd, austere, promising, inadequate, awkward, chancy, and often gang up, inflaming heated quarrels and fiery—

I recalled, this moment, the sight of red-hot molten glass ready to be blown by human or mechanical breath and shaped into drinking glasses, bottles, stemware, vases, decorative crystal objects. I saw this process happen at the Corning Glass factory that I toured many years ago on a tenth-grade class trip. We were on our way back to New York after visiting Gettysburg and the Bethlehem Steel works. We must have stopped at other historic and instructive places, but those are the three I remember seeing on that trip. Fire figures in those three places, from rifles and furnaces. The glass-blowing fire is the one I prefer to envision, the other two sites were tragic and fearsome. Perhaps my memory of the work at Corning is vivid because, soon after I was there, I blew glass myself, using a Bunsen burner in our school's crafts room. Misshapen lumps are what I produced, after many attempts, but trying was the point. It is still the point.

I should strive to make my work transparent: small glass windows, solidly framed, easily openable. The windowpanes should be uncluttered, no muntins, no curtains or shades. The windows should face north for steady daylight without the sun's flashy dazzle. The glass should be free of cracks and bubbles that distort vision and coherence. Every window should be clean as a whistle, no streaky residue of dust or absurdity missed by a polishing, wondrously clear, a sight stripped bare by its observer.

I don't have much luck accommodating all of those insistent shoulds, not even such likelihood.

Which doesn't stop me from sitting in a weatherworn dinghy, fishing for clarity, day after day until maybe, occasionally, I land it.

Surrounding Conditions

A quip, long submerged, surfaced unaccountably this morning as a dead goldfish does in a glass bowl, belly up and stinking: "A woman is only a woman, but a good cigar is a smoke." I occasionally heard my father quote that line, which he told me was from a poem by Kipling, whose *Just So Stories* I loved. My father was a big Kipling fan. He was also a cigar smoker.

That noxious punch line didn't bother me until I neared adolescence. Younger, I never felt there was anything objectionable about the overhanging haze of cigar smoke in our living room, nothing irritating about the red-and-gold cigar bands my father gave me to wear on my fingers and that I would have put through my nose and earlobes if I could have, nothing belittling about his frequent requests that I fetch and use a silent butler to empty his cut-glass ashtray. Cigar smells colonized his clothes, his hair, lingered in our home's upholstery and atmosphere, sweet and harsh at once, durable and ephemeral, appealing and off-putting. Those contradictory qualities were puzzling but not troublesome, perhaps because they were so familiar.

My father smoked Havanas; this was before the United States embargo on Cuban exports. The cigars were individually encased in metal tubes. He stored a supply of them in a humidor at Dunhill's on Fifth Avenue, near his office. He once took me to Dunhill's, I was nine or ten, on vacation from school and visiting his office, where I was kept busy for an hour or so crawling on the floor and picking up tiny diamonds that dropped under and around the table where my palsied grandfather sat. Magnifying loupe in one shaky hand, extra-long tweezers in the other, my grandfather sorted polished stones into piles on a white desk blotter, then wrapped each pile in a separate *briefke*, a little two-layered packet of folded glossy papers, which was when the dropping occurred. It was work that kept him busy and going, though it had to be redone by a steadier sharper-sighted person in the family business. My father detoured to Dunhill's on our way to his daily lunch place. When he opened his humidor and I saw those shiny tubes stacked like torpedoes in a warship's bomb compartment, I thought: Will they kill him? They didn't, as it turned out.

A few years later, the cruelty of Kipling's line dawned on me. It was foul, not funny, a putrid wisecrack about women. I would be a woman soon. Would I be considered as immaterial as the smoke a cigar produced? Would I be labeled a good smoke or a middling one or stogie-cheap? Would I glow steadily or fizzle out fast? Time might answer my questions, but I could not.

This morning's rotten fish is still floating here, reeking. I picture myself coolly picking it up by its forked tail and flushing it down a toilet into the ideological sewer where it belongs, where women a mere handful of years younger than I am are quick to dispose of it actually, publicly, loudly, with the sure and vigorous outcry of their new-model imperatives. My innate and acquired behavioral codes do not include outcrying in public.

I came of age at a time when most women were quietly complying with signals they received from powerful cultural transmitters operating after World War II. Peppy muscular skilled Rosie the Riveter and the norm-busting wartime workforce of over eighteen million American women had vanished in a misty bog of renounced pathfinders. Marriage, motherhood, and housewifery were the crystal-clear messages sent in the 1950s. A short while later, the customary ground rules changed, thanks to yeasty upheavals of activism that energized overdue legitimate protests about varied injustices and outrages. Seemly lockjaw was no longer the default mode for women, who had voices and used them. Among other important causes, women fought resoundingly for rights that would redefine their roles and horizons. Some battles were won, others lost, some are still being fought. I marched only once, for Roe v. Wade, accompanied by one of my daughters, my twin sisters, and a niece. Otherwise, I didn't go to rallies or join protest marchers, even when I sided with their causes. There is something in me that doesn't love a parade, a mass rally, a political demonstration. That something is, in brief, my story.

There are broader heavier stories than my refugee's tale of internalized outsiderhood, a vast and fast-growing number of contemporary memoirs and historical accounts that reveal adversities I never had, delve into burdens, mentalities, injuries, regimes, and dangers that far out-weigh what is in my little tote bag of experience. I can speculate about those larger narratives, graze on schol-arly meat and its sprigs of documentation, notionally see a blurry sfumato painting of how things were and felt in other circumstances or times, but much of that strikes me as spurious, an exercise in making-believe. I know the truths of one story, and I know they are unreliable, a loosely-stitched fabric of authentic, selective, and false memories, patches of fact, emotional twine, fluffy hunches, some misperceptions. Even so, even suspect, not unique or generally gripping, it is a story I own. That it deters me from marching and demonstrating is a given I live with, another received signal, that one trans-mitted in human smoke.

I have smoke on the brain today, redundant systems of acrid cloudy air running my engine of thought. Cigar fogs and smoke signals, sfumato images of past and present realities, the whiff of a putrid joke about women, swampy mists shrouding milestones of abandoned paths, the smoking gun of deliberately picked or partially concocted memories. I accidentally on purpose forgot, we used to say when I wore cigar-band rings on my fingers, a lame alibi for ignoring our basic training of honesty. I never heard my children say that or, more recently, my grand-children; every generation hatches it own chirpy sloppy excuses. Slimy birdshit fell from the sky onto my hair this morning when I was taking my daily early morn-ing walk. "Only connect!" was E. M. Forster's emphatic advice about life, passion, and the piecemeal business of writing. I am in a thick miasma of disjunction here, now, snatching glimpses, clutching at flux. Smoke and smells dissipate, sparkling diamonds cascade from rocky hands, birds fly off, written histories are changing era-driven constructs, sewage drains away, memory slips, boundar-ies shift, minds drift, and I can't ground those volatile fragments. The links elude me today, the instrumental hooks and hinges of solid connection.

Maybe I could recharge the stalled engine, get going again, in another clearer direction, perhaps. I don't know what I may stumble on, let alone where I'll land up. For me, this is a hit-or-mostly-miss line of work. I wish it were a science with a strict methodology ensuring the possibility of repeatable results. Science. There's a jump-start for now, a flash bolting out of the blue.

The so-called hard sciences are largely beyond me. I know a little about some softer ones, information sporadically accrued in the passage of time. I also know a couple of languages, have on-the-job training in familial, marital, parental, and social arbitration, some geopolitical and historic knowledge, extensive domestic savvy, scraps of medical specifics, a satisfactory acquaintance with literature written in English, a cache of personal lore, and a dependable forehand crosscourt drop shot. These varied bodies of learning, along with some others I sopped up by osmosis over the years, are a useful source of ideas, skills, questions, words, constraints, choices, doubts, and more. I appreciate and use the nourishing mix routinely provided by my different educations, but I find myself stealing mouthfuls of a language I never learned.

My several vocabularies worked well enough for many years, and still do. I have yet to meet an adult who could not talk weather or food or local and national politics. With health, the economy, children, terrorism, the environment, elderly ailing parents, new electronic gadgetry, sports, television and movies as additional go-to topics, there is no conversation you can not make with most people. All the same, I now feel the lack of scientific education, not because I want to talk science but because I sometimes use its vivid and alluring language in my work and would like to understand, more or less, what the words mean.

I am not pleased to be so squarely located on one side of what C. P. Snow famously and controversially called "the two cultures" of humanities and sciences. The single-sex college I attended was strong on the liberal arts, skittish in regard to women doing science, in those long-ago lower-tech days anyhow, and most of us arrived there already tuned to that dissonance. I didn't lack curiosity about the science side, but I never had the nerve, or ability perhaps, to straddle that big gap. So I make do now with smatterings of scientific knowledge, some hunches, a heap of misconceptions, and lists of interesting words that crop up from time to time.

For instance, here are a few of the terms I spotted in Tuesday science sections of *The New York Times* or heard on television nature and science programs over the past several years and jotted down for their suggestive potential. Extremophile; confidence interval; founder effect; civil dawn; point of magnetic indifference; selfish genes; sentinel event; a theory of everything; truth-maintenance systems; event horizon; starved coastlines; charmed quarks; calculus of pleasure; punctuated equilibrium; polar wander. I know what makes these words click for me, but I don't know what most of them actually describe and convey about the physical or mathematical or biological and other workings of our world and its universe. I tell myself that the click is what counts, for my small purposes. I tell myself a number of things I don't believe and can't defend but continue to do and to feel as a matter of course.

I find it hard to believe that I persist in working on a tightrope without a net of factual rigor. I don't trust my faith in the powers of language to keep me from mis-stepping and plunging into the emptiness of yet another flunked attempt. I am chronically skeptical about the worth of what I think I think. I fault myself for skulking behind an "I" on paper. I feel seriously uneasy about perpetrating deceptions under the smoke screen of anecdotal license. If I had even the impermanent strength of smoke, I'd crush these jarring qualms by resolving to quit the fishy work I do.

Back, back to fish where this spin through time and ambient fogs began, whirling me to misgivings.

Clocks and calendars turn in fixed and unsurprising rotations. My circling here, now, is incidental, a passing sphere in the everyday disarray of miscellaneous odds and ends. Chancy and fugitive as it may be, the shape is clear, whole, and momentarily stationary: a zero at rest in the onrush and fullness of life. "The rest is silence" were the dying words of an epic self-doubter. I can believe that.

Object Lessons

here are three little monkeys squatting on a glass shelf above the sink in my bathroom, a gift from a friend several years ago. They are made of soap, and so are subject to erosion by the inevitable clouds of moisture in a small enclosed place where hot showers are taken daily. Their facial features and hands have lost some edges, their knees are mere suggestions of former contours, their elbows still have jab potential. Despite their impaired condition, I have not considered evicting these squatters. I like even the diminished material presence of their ancient proverbial wisdom: See, hear, speak no evil. I wish I could claim those watchwords in regard to my own behavior, but that would be terminally pipe-dreamy.

Other eloquent things are present and visible in my home. On one of the kitchen counters there is a row of fourteen old tin boxes, caddies, and canisters of different sizes and shapes, all printed with colorful images and slogans that relate to their original contents. Over the years, I found these containers by chance, in thrift shops, at street fairs and yard sales, in pseudo-antique stores. I keep spaghetti in a tall round can, other tins hold tea bags, lentils, cocoa powder, bullion cubes, almonds, and similar nonperishables. I use what is and what is not in those containers, all decorative, none valuable, except for the intangible nostalgia, personal and cultural, that I store in them.

One of those containers is a slightly bent time-scarred can of Bon Ami with its trademark picture of a chick newly popped out of its shell, the brand of scouring powder that my mother used. Did she choose and stick with that brand in connection with the four infants she popped out of her body? Or did its name prompt wishful moments as she cleaned the sink, the tub, the gritty powder dissolving on her wet rubber-gloved hands, slipping out of her grasp as she envisioned . . . what? More good friends? Closer ones like those she had in girlhood, in another country, on a different continent? A fresher spotless life? Dependable strength? Timeproof personal luster? These are questions she would not have answered if I had asked them, she would have promptly dismissed them as outlandish, invasive, and uncouth: a trifecta of negatives.

I am still searching for a vintage can I would like to have, Old Dutch Cleanser. A few are available online, but I firmly believe that not looking for and finding one fortuitously would be cheating. I used to hear my father talking Dutch to his five siblings when I was a child. His family left Belgium to pass the years of World War I in neutral Holland, and Dutch remained the language they liked speaking to each other. I have a photo of him skating on a frozen canal, arm in arm with his youngest sister, he looks about thirteen, pleased with his ease on ice, with the support he is giving his little sister, with the sunny day, the exhilarating sport, with anything and everything, his wide smile hints. Which could be why the Old Dutch can speaks to me, why it says: Find me, look at me, keep me close by.

Despite its absence from my array of old tins, I often picture, crystal-clearly, Old Dutch's trademark image of a woman wearing a white apron and headdress and red sabots, chasing invisible dirt with an upraised stick, and I hear it ringing like an alarm clock: time to clean up, clear away, get on with it.

A notional linkage of parents and household scouring powder may not be far-fetched. Both groups are gentle for the most part, some more abrasive, others not up to the job, few are damagingly harsh, a tiny number are toxic, even fewer are deadly. Although at the time it was happening I did not appreciate the friction of my parents' efforts to ready me for the future, scrubbing my behavior until it sparkled according to their lights, cleansing my mind of mistaken and worthless ideas, verbally sluicing the surplus pounds off my adolescent body, it did prepare me for the life they expected I would, I should have. Apart from their formative and retained European leanings, and the mechanical novelties and up-to-date outlooks produced by the passage of time, my adult life approximates the one they envisioned for me, not radically different from their own in America. However, I eventually took on a secondary life, one they never foresaw: a writer's daily and elusive doings.

If I were to call my work self a cleaning product, it might be Comet, for my ongoing attempts to streak paths of light across the infinite empty skies of a computer screen. Alternatively, more reliably, I could be Dawn, rising daily to soap and rinse my mind's sink and utensils with vivid sunshine. My children might label me Arm & Hammer, not these days, but for the repetitious comments I made about their teenage behavior, most of which they heard as irritating pounding. That was then, now is a different story, more like Windex, for mutual multi-purpose sparkle.

Tin cans aside, I have a small miscellany of evocative personal effects, most I acquired myself, a few parentally sourced, none I use these days, none rare or costly. That trove consists of the key for my old metal roller skates, a garter belt, a chrome cigarette case, a portable typewriter and several boxes of ribbons for it, a Mercury dime from the year of my birth, a red Bakelite umbrella-shaped stand with slots for six yellow-handled fruit knives, a box of floppy disks, an ivory glove-finger stretcher for ladies' kid gloves, a half-filled S&H Green Stamps booklet, a tapestry reticule on a metal chain, and a russet-and-ocher striped vintage Oshkosh valise I found in my mother's guest room closet when I was emptying her apartment after she died. It is monogrammed J.B.S., her initials, and formerly contained letters handwritten on tissue-thin paper, my parents' correspondence during the six months of their engagement when they were mostly apart, she in Vienna and he worldwide on business trips. I must have had the conscience of a turnip when I threw out those letters because they were written in German, the language of a nation I categorically unapologetically shun. Everyone has a sticking point, or several, and that is one of mine.

I keep those previously useful or decorative things because, like the emblematic stripes on the valise, they semaphore bygone times. I often wonder if I am guilty of packaging free-floating anxiety as sentimental keepsakes. Whatever the case, I will continue to house those objects as solid reminders of inevitable ephemerality: of life, of obsoleted ideas and machinery, social and cultural outlooks and pursuits, methods of learning and communication, of prior years and relationships, an entire universe of what was, my own small world also, friends and hopes I had and lost, promises I kept and didn't, what I missed, what I wanted, what I wasted, what I can't retrieve.

Monkeys in the bathroom, kitchen line-up of old cans, and garter belt in a bureau drawer are only a few of the meaningful things in the apartment I live in with my husband, mementos similar to those accumulated by many people in their homes. Infants' knitted booties are one sort of memory-jogger, varsity jackets are another, as are old address books and diaries, wedding invitations, photographs, diplomas, military discharge papers, theater and concert programs, lapsed drivers' licenses and passports; the list of more and less treasurable material possessions is long. Arbitrarily, I exclude artworks from this roster of prized belongings, except for those made at a young age by a family member: paper clip chainwork necklaces, drawings of heavy-headed flowers, dinosaur stickers on cutwork paper doilies, that sort of guileless art.

Because I am subject to frequent fevers of neatness, I often dust and tidy the things I like to see in our home, and to rearrange every now and then. I have my share of the memorabilia mentioned above, but most of it is out of sight in storage spaces. There are things I enjoy looking at daily, such as a bevy of blue-and-white beauties, four pottery pitchers and a teapot, but I seldom risk handling them as they are perched on a narrow glass shelf. The books I am pleased to see in every room but the bathrooms don't need attention beyond an occasional flick of a feather duster or clap of their covers, they are and stay orderly, parked side by side on shelves. The piano in our living room, unplayed for decades, its keys warped, its sounding board cracked, continues to make music for my eyes. The furniture throughout the apartment doesn't particularly stir me, nor do I move it. The many family photos on display are a different matter, notably engaging and expressive, but difficult to rearrange. I have to decide to consider or ignore several factors: when the photos were taken, the clear visibility of faces and background places, an occasion's importance, the allure or triviality of the image, and whether or not it is time to change the photos, see the same people at different ages in different settings.

A few days ago, walking through a narrow corridor in our apartment that has a five-generation exhibit of framed family photos on its crowded walls, I stopped in the middle of that passageway, abruptly wondering, and not for the first time, how or even if I will be seen when the youngest people in those photos, my grandchildren, have grandchildren.

For one, I probably won't be seen on paper in a wooden, metal, leather or plastic frame placed on a flat surface or hung on a wall, though I might be spotted on pages in a photo album, if such a thing continues to be kept, looked at, possibly even cherished.

Secondly, I may be out of sight, prints of photographs in which I appear having been scanned, digitized, and filed with newer digital photos of me, all of them sent to a vast depot of virtual snapshots with that file inadvertently mislabeled: unclaimable and irreplaceable lost baggage.

Thirdly, unlike pictorial trademarks on commercial products, my image will not hint at my contents or their usage. Seeing me isn't knowing me. A photographic likeness is only that: a similarity, not the real thing. Even so, simply allusive, a printed photo speaks volumes, and is worth having, keeping, seeing from time to time, freshly or as previously, its particulars don't change, light and the person looking are the variable essentials.

Like many people, I have looked at many photographs over the years: old and recent ones, amateur candids and professional work, landscapes, portraits, architectural views, nudes, streetscapes, all sorts of seen, snapped, and printed observations made by one person in a particular place at a specific time, incomplete but generally credible glimpses of people, an event, a place, more or less informative.

I like the breadth of details in photographs. They often reveal something I never noticed. Reading photographs, like reading a passerby's glance, a room, a book, a natural or man-made vista, has enlarged and changed some of my views, and I get to sightsee lives of people I never met and places I never visited.

Along with the imagery, I like the lingo of photography and cinematography. Candid. Transparency. Positive. Blow-up. Available light. Proof. Mug shot. Exposure. Shadowgraph. Answer Print. Establishing shot. Key light. Close-up. Follow shot. Fill light. Some of those terms could apply to writing, what to aim for anyhow. Others identify themselves in their own words. Several baffle me, but I don't investigate their meanings, I enjoy the sound of their secrets.

Secrecy and I have a life-long relationship that is not a romance. In childhood, decoding the silence about the war my family escaped was an important hush-hush job

I undertook, and largely failed. Nor was I successful in adolescence, working alone and undercover, tailing the elusive norms of teenage behavior, bodily and social. Older, I habitually kept my secrets to myself, as characteristically private people do. These days, writing personal essays, I have to disclose some of my inside information, render it in words on paper, efforts that frequently result in wild goose chases and an overworked delete key. Still, I choose to write essays: attempts. So I keep trying. Giving up would be fleeing from my own war, the skirmishes I wage with words, advancing, retreating, changing tactics, constantly striving for cogent outcomes, clear and convincing.

Clarity is not a regular feature of my working hours. I sometimes feel that my mind resembles the La Brea Tar Pits, fossilized memories and ideas lurking out of sight and reach in a dark bog of the past. Other mornings, I see it as a usually well-stocked supermarket with its shelves depleted by panic buying in the murky daylight of a fast-approaching Category Four hurricane. There are hours when the desk in my workroom suddenly, unaccountably, becomes a blackout zone of radio silence from the transmitter in my head. And then there are the occasional sunny days, blue cloudless skies, a breeze of words I don't have to search for or struggle with, they glide on the air, land in my mind, on my hands, tapping and tapping, recording their presence as they arrive and amount to something grounded, something plausible and accessible.

That's a tall order, but it gets filled occasionally, often enough for me to keep trying. "A" for effort, at the least.

Sometimes I think about abandoning that effort, breaking my habit of thinking things through on paper, stopped traipsing through my memories, swore off overloading mere notions with my baggage, quit probing the relevance of my hunches, retired from wrestling with words. Would my mind shuffle to indolence? stagnation? fogginess as a prelude to feeble? Or would it shift to routinely taking hesitation waltz steps: a momentary pause, then a glide? This is a dance step I am learning to do, willy-nilly.

As of today, and despite the random pauses, I won't consider exit strategies until the thought of quitting becomes a blaring alarm bell or an irresistible siren song. It is not yet more than a whisper on a passing breath of air.

The Persistence of Yellow

Some years ago my husband and I went plot shopping, a sensible project for people our age, one then nearing senior citizenship and the other already there. We wanted to explore our options, make an informed decision about buying our last shared bed. We did not think our shopping was morbid, laced as it was with a jigger of strong *eau de vie*. Nor did we believe we were tempting fate, as genuinely superstitious people believe they are doing if they speak the name of a disease or mention an event they dread. Buying our plot was another sort of retirement plan to make, one for the uncharted future. Over the years we talked about looking for a burial site, but kept putting it off. We had lawyer-written wills, signed durable powers of attorney, designated healthcare proxies, and a notarized statement of our final wishes, all the legal planning that people are advised to do for the possible decline of competence and the predictable end of life. Still, those formal documents were merely intentional: abstract preparations. It was time to ground one of our plans in the concrete. We had to find a cemetery we liked.

Cremation is unacceptable to us. We are abidingly mindful of the furnaces in the death camps. My husband's family, the survivors in it, is buried in northeastern France in an old Jewish cemetery that used to have towering old pines lining its gravel paths. All of those venerable trees were uprooted by the powerful freak windstorm that ripped a corridor of destruction through England and Western Europe in December of 1999. A rogue storm savaging that part of the world is highly suggestive but I'll leave it at that, refrain from looking at the monstrous figure in history's carpet. I am squinting at a much smaller area rug, skimpy and finite.

My family, all but a lone twig of it, lies in a cemetery in suburban New Jersey, in a section reserved for people who belong to an Orthodox burial society. That cemetery is a flat grassy place, largely treeless and blatantly functional. It is surrounded by visible and audible strip malls, office plazas, housing developments, parking lots, and busy highways, the landscape of actual and aspirational mobility in America, a dynamic that was permanently foreign to my clan of refugees, to its elders anyhow, whose mutual seclusiveness was masked as self-sufficiency. At a stone's throw, from across Montefiore Avenue that runs by it, that one section of the cemetery resembles my notional picture of a *shtetl* before the populations of those villages perished: plain neat narrow houses shoulder to shoulder on narrow dirt paths. Up close, the impression is reinforced, many of the names on the tombstones are Polish, the texts in Hebrew, the birth and death dates in accordance with the Jewish calendar. Only recently did that burial society partially acknowledge the 21st century by allowing men and women to be laid to rest in adjoining graves; women are still not permitted to stand next to men during a burial's ritual graveside prayers. Once a year I like to visit my gender-gapped relatives in that little gray village, but I wouldn't want to live in it, so to speak. When I see their graves, I often imagine missing the company of my parents and extended family, and they missing mine, dust whispering to nearby dust, asking where on earth I was, why I chose to distance myself from them. Invariably, I wonder if any future visitors would recall me and my place in that familial scheme of things without my name on a tombstone there to see and to mark with pebbles. Even so, my husband and I positively agreed on our need for a different cemetery.

We headed for the hills of Westchester. Pioneering, we called it, though we scouted the region many years earlier and settled a bit of it with a house in the northern reaches of that county. Westchester's proximity to Manhattan is a plus for us on the weekends we drive to our house, additionally enhanced by the features of the area's glacially-formed terrain. We like the look of rolling ridges, now-wooded drumlins, kames and eskers, the numerous ponds created by stranded blocks of ancient ice melting in place, the occasional erratic boulder perched where it doesn't appear to belong, the overall green of it bordered by the Hudson River on one side and the Long Island Sound on the other.

Most of the cemeteries are in lower Westchester, closer to the city whose dead and mourners they serve. On several Sunday winter afternoons, driving back to Manhattan, we detoured to a handful of them. If they looked okay in raw weather, they would be fine in time. We called ahead for appointments with their custodians who could steer us to available plots. We checked out the plantings, the styles of the monuments and markers, the neighbors, the views, the space between graves, the slope of a site for natural drainage, the light and potential shade, selling price and upkeep costs—comparison shopping, as though and in fact for a downsized new home, and in a gated community to boot. Kensico, the largest and most picturesque garden cemetery of those we saw, seemed wrong for us, too country-clubby, too squarely located in Valhalla, a hamlet named for the heavenly home of mythic heroes slain in battles that were not ours, not our myths either. Ferncliff, Mount Hope, and Mount Pleasant were among the others we visited, none of them quite filling the bill, vague as it was. We knew what we didn't like, but what precisely we wanted was unclear, an inkling at best.

One bleak February afternoon we went to Mount Eden Cemetery. The caretaker wasn't busy, no burials were scheduled, we were the only folks he'd seen all day, he reported. He offered to walk around with us, he wanted to stretch his legs. We preferred to wander privately but it was hard to refuse his offer, especially after he sweetened it by volunteering to make us a cup of tea. That we did turn down. We walked the grounds for what felt like hours, time dilated by his tortoiselike pace. We had plodded to the top of what can be called a mount only in generous hyperbole when he pointed out an available grave site that seemed to already have our name on it. It has the same western exposure as our house up-county, about the same elevation providing a big open view of a hilly horizon, a similar quietness accented by the frequent and plaintive tooting of a Metro North commuter train. The caretaker said we shouldn't delay a decision because "plots are going like hotcakes." Those were his very words, and they did the job.

In the office there, we wrote and signed a request for adjoining double plots on that site, room for growth. We have three children, two have children of their own. None of them live near New York. Making final arrangements for them would definitely be unwelcome micromanagement, and certifiably premature. However, on the chance that our still-single son might some day think about being buried beside us, extra space would come in handy. He became an observant Jew several years ago, a factor influencing our choice that we recognized only midway through our subtractive process of plot shopping. Mount Eden respects the laws of the Sabbath, is closed to burials and visitors on Saturdays.

The following day we phoned the administrative director of Mount Eden and firmed up our request with a credit card deposit. A week later, our deposit became a cash purchase, no installment plans allowed. Three weeks after that, we received a deed of ownership, a map detailing our site's lot-lines, a two-page statement of the cemetery corporation's rules and regulations pertaining to the acceptable burial procedures of plot owners, the conduct of visitors, and the planting of property. Also enclosed was a schedule of yearly charges for maintenance and perpetual-care fees, expenses deferrable until a plot is occupied. This packet of information is still in its original manila envelope, stowed in a cardboard box in a storage closet in our apartment, out of sight but not out of mind, mine for one, at present.

I opened that box last week to look for my husband's and my own Social Security cards and our birth certificates, mine issued in Belgium, his in France. These are two of the many documents required when applying for a new Real ID compliant driver's license. I found what I needed for our appointment next week at the DMV, then passed a couple of hours rambling through the past, reading a variety of old and newer documents: diplomas, my husband's Air Force discharge papers, a copy of our marriage license and the *ketubah* my parents insisted on, a few recently expired desk calendars kept for no useful reason but my mild discomfort at the thought of junking people's names and the festive events recorded on those pages, the passenger list of the ocean liner on which I emigrated to America, some evaluations of our children's behavioral

and academic qualities as observed by their elementary
school teachers, handwritten genealogies of our two families going back five generations, those kinds of personal
papers, another scheme of things in which I have a place.
I had a good time, those hours in bygone years. Memories whirled around me, some spontaneous and some
rehearsed, stomping a vigorous polka to the beat of sys-
tole, diastole. It felt as though I had crashed a costume
party being held in a clearing in a forest of papery trees
of life; come as you were. I was sorry about having to
shelve the box and get back to my here-and-now self and
doings, but knowing I could revisit those papers whenever I want to subdue the hounds of regret. And then, just
before I closed the box, I spotted the manila envelope sent
by Mount Eden at the bottom it. Good night, goodbye,
farewell, the party was over with a bang: the prospect of
death pounding on my door.

I haven't been able to shake that thought since I saw
that envelope last week. I tried to loosen its grip by dwell-
ing on the pragmatic stuff of arrangements, family, place,
weather, geology, property, documentation. I failed.

It is not surprising that death is on my mind these days,
even without a push from a cemetery's mailing. Two people
I cherish are in the jaws of illnesses from which they are
not likely to be yanked. If only sickness could be beaten
with a loud authoritative No!

What I should say is "Nuts!" if a serious illness attacks
me. That was Brigadier General McAuliffe's terse defiant

reply to German emissaries demanding that American forces surrender the besieged town of Bastogne during the Battle of the Bulge. The encircled Americans held the town, won that fight, and subsequent battles. Nuts! to giving in, giving up, getting beaten. I hope to be brave enough to believe that and act accordingly if the need arises.

For the time being, I am a visitor to hospital rooms, doctors' waiting rooms, home sickbeds, or I visit by phone, make chatty calls, do what I can, not much, to momentarily distract the minds of people with one thing looming large in their thinking.

There is no way to tenderize the thought of dying for easier chewing and digestion. Inevitable as death is, we don't have a secular handle on its unreportable aftermath, I don't anyhow. I can't sort or construe baffling nonbeing. If its meaning could be found in books on a reading list for the mother of all courses, Mastering Death, I would study those books, cram for the final, though I'd never find out how I did on that exam. If I could posit a theory of everything that accounted for the mysteries of death's universe, I would. If I were a reader of the Talmud, I could turn to Maimonides to deliver me from perplexity. If I were a doctor as my husband is, I would be accustomed to confronting mortality, know how to grapple with it, where to outflank it, when to surrender, battle strategies that don't figure in von Clausewitz's military treatise. If. If is wishful on a low-fat diet. Alternatively, if is life reduced to its bare chanciness.

So far, so lucky is my personal watchword now. Should my luck run out, "Nuts!" would be the best response.

It would also be deeply uncharacteristic. The mere thought of death and its vast dark uncertainties makes my naturally yellow bones clatter like maracas, I can feel them clacking an alert: Back off, stay safe, stick with the familiar dazzle and blur of life. Again, once again on these pages, I am refraining from looking at something I probably should tackle, even fearfully. This is shaping up as an agenda of items I don't dare to put on the table for consideration.

Sometimes, this moment, it feels as though I write on a fault zone. There are fractures on my narrative crust, evidence of continental plates moving and shearing below the surface, of seismic events waiting to happen, maybe the Big One, as Californians call it. I record the observable impacts of small quakes that rattle or uplift me, but I avoid, too often, the underlying trouble areas. I think about firing myself from a job I don't always do through and through, from the inside out; my second thought regularly is: I do what I can, how and when I want, I am on my own here, shaky and whistling in the dark, alone with the say-so.

So: to something else that rattles me, the slippage of memory. This concern is as age-appropriate as shopping for a plot, the process as subtractive as our search was, but that's it for similarities. There's no choice in the matter of memory loss, no fixed lot-lines or schedule of human costs, no contractual guarantees between a mind and the brain that runs it, no escape clause either. Confusion is too flimsy a word for what happens to people with severe cognitive impairments. This is knowledge I acquired empirically and would rather forget, but can't. I can't gag the nagging memory of my father and the punches that decked him in his unfair fight with a dementing disease. Affection and the passage of time haven't softened that shrill remembrance for me, I live with it "as is," the brusque caveat on labels attached to used or damaged goods in yard sales and at auctions.

I remember many things I would rather forget, and vice versa, but it's the new and random blank moments that concern me. Thankfully, they are still only pesky, impish enough to play with me. I am the "it" searching for names, words, previous events, plans, addresses, and mostly finding what I seek, tagging the hiders before they sprint to home base in my gray matter, free to elude me again. As of today, I can shrug off my transient lapses.

Today may diminish to never when and if mild forgetfulness advances to firm, and firm in time to tyrannical. I am afraid that will happen to me. Along with being a medalist in the Olympics of avoidance, I am a born catastrophist; the two habits of mind are related, raised together, sibs in trepidation. My sense of vulnerability may be ancestral, a trait encoded in my genes, or it might be circumstantial, the result of being born in a particular place in a specific year, or it could just be me, always conscious of the tiny "r" turning scared into scarred. A lowercase r looks like an upside-down fishhook. I try to keep clear of the baited barb but at times I feel compelled or obligated to bite, and then I am snagged for hours, thrashing on the business end of a strong taut line that unreels from the historic past and my childhood terror about the blue numbers I saw on forearms.

My chronic wariness is another choiceless matter, or I would have opted for daring in place of cold feet a long time ago. "If your *oma* had wheels she'd be a tram," my mother used to say, a *Mitteleuropean* version of pigs sprouting wings to fly with, as impossible as choosing to be fearless, as unreal.

One reality is that I can still spell backwards without hesitating. Spelling backwards is a standard part of tests given to people whose mental acuity is in question. How can the ability to spell in reverse on demand measure anything but a person's knack for speedy U-turns? Able was I ere I saw Elba. A man, a plan, a canal, Panama. Dlrow. Elpoep. Efil. Daerd. Htaed. Gnihton. Easy, duck soup, a game, for now.

Now is this bright October afternoon, this golden hour that has the allure of a scenic pullout on a road that leads more or less directly to an airless dark destination. Even passingly, interruptively, blank-mindedly, the panoramic vista rates a look. The sky is blue, the day is seasonably warm, the view is grand, my luck is holding, and I am stopping here, now, because I can, I want to, I say so, taking in the scenery, basking in this sunny moment before darkness falls.

Pages from a Daybook

I needed a pillow last night from the closet in the room that was my daughter's until she married. That closet now stores boxes of old photos, deflated air mattresses, a soccer ball, a carton of vinyl LPs, blankets, and more. It also houses a pair of her pink ballet slippers with their ribbons tied together and dangling from a hook near the door. Whenever I see them I recall a dream she had and described to me. She was seven, having difficulties with her handwriting, and woke one morning smiling, elated. "I dreamed I was the god of letters," she said. "All the letters were on the blanket at the end of my bed, waiting for me to tell them what to do. Whatever I said they exactly did, like pliés and positions and arabesques for me to copy into words. Then I woke up."

I stole a version of her dream for myself eight years after she had it, definitely without the divinity feature.

Like those ballet slippers, I am also mostly in the dark, but temporarily: the hours I pass at my desk. Mine is a dark of a different order, although a light bulb can illuminate both of them, one visibly and one cartoonishly, comic-strip style. That latter bulb has an electricity of its own, goes on or off, flickers, dims, flares, gleams. Occasionally, but not dependably, it throws a clear steady light on what I need to see. Or it may turn opaque, buzz, and shatter, fragmenting useless ideas. Either way, I appreciate its help.

What to do next is always a dilemma. Which recollection or new notion will pop up to engross me for hours, days, longer? What might be generally interesting or topical or quirkily intriguing or clearly, promptly, forgettable?

Forgetting is general. Everyone does it, more or less.

Sometimes I think that my memory and I could have traveled with the Donner Party. I cannibalize it for nourishment that keeps me going, step by unpredictable step, to some fresh and maybe broader views of our shared years, skin, contents, circumstances, destination. It eats itself, slowly and piecemeal at present, but could chew and swallow faster, or it won't, there's no predicting.

The cannibal likeness may be allusive overkill, but for me it has the heft of an experiential finding, a rule of thumb that works for and against me. Although I can't control some of my memory's choices or its pace of self-consumption, I can often use the images, feelings, words, and ideas it offers, or I can redirect them, urge my memory to go feed somewhere else.

I should get up and go! Away from this desk and its indifferent machinery, from my misbegotten unsustainable attempts, the trackless paths to nowhere, mere hints and muddled get-on-with-it ploys, failures I have trouble acknowledging, away from all of that for now and into the hubbub of the metropolis around me, the nourishing clamor and pull of the actual world.

The weekly science section dropped out of the newspaper when I picked it up at our door yesterday, and I saw a front-page headline mention of the dark-sky paradox, a term I never encountered before. I didn't stop to read the article, but got to it in the evening. That phrase has to do with why the night sky is dark when there are so many stars lighting it. Paradoxical indeed, and that's about all I gleaned from the article with its scientific verbiage and complex diagrams. The terse phrase will remain a mystery to me, literally over my head.

It feels as though I am on sentry duty these days, patrolling the perimeters of a battlefield where two of my friends are combating serious illnesses. I can almost hear myself shouting Halt! Who goes there? I would have to be certifiably chowderheaded not to connect the dots between Who goes there? and Am I next? I have my share of unsensible qualms and characterological flaws, but obtuseness is not among them. That being so, I can't ignore the cogency of the loud inner voice I hear, or the threat of that battleground where my personal heroes are fighting, where others already fought and fell.

There was an old Ojibwa dreamcatcher in the window of a gallery on East 67th Street that I walked by yesterday afternoon. I spotted it just as the crosstown bus rumbled by, lurched to a halt on the corner, and I sprinted to catch the bus. I should have stopped, paid some attention to that suggestive artifact. I know it wouldn't do for me what it does in Native American tribal belief and traditional usage as a protective charm that dispels any evil spirits present in the air or in the mind, often hung over cradle boards. Even without the least dissipation of the several disturbing thoughts and images on my mind, I should have given that beautiful object, a thin wooden hoop framing a spider-like web of string ornamented with colored beads and dangling feathers, more of my time, more than a glance, more on-the-spot musing about webs of safety, the magic of enduring traditions, feathered flyaway dreams and hopes, not sit here poking at today's soggy leftovers of should-haves. I wasn't going anywhere special anyhow.

I was skittish when I started writing several decades ago, spooked by my new expressive shortfalls, reminders of early childhood difficulties I had with English, my second language. These days I throw caution to the winds when I write, conceptual caution that is, typing is not skydiving. Away from my desk, I am not daring. Today's menu choice for my pre-work frame of mind was scrambled jitters with side of—

Time for lunch.

On my walk in the park this morning, I saw a Kousa dogwood in full and pristine bloom. Its top looked like a crown of fresh white flowers, something brides might wear, and reminded me of a picture I snapped of my mother in a fancy hat on her way to a party. This was in my career as a budding shutterbug. My birthday present from my parents when I turned ten was a Brownie box camera. "Take your life," my father said as he handed me the camera. I was shocked, then terrified. Did he think I might kill myself? A family friend had taken his life a few months earlier, I overheard whispers about that terrible event. My father must have recognized the fear on my face, because then he told me to take pictures of my daily life, friends, my school, our apartment, the city streets, the soda counter in the Lido Pharmacy where I spent the coins that I stole from his coat pockets in the hall closet. I knew my thefts weren't a secret, or the point of what he said.

The Brownie had a face, two round eyes above a big round nose, no mouth though, unless you consider its printed results to be eloquent. After I learned how to load and unload rolls of film without exposing them to ruin, I poked that big nose into my life and more public business. I dropped the Brownie on a sidewalk one rainy afternoon,

accidentally damaging it beyond repair, and ending my
eight-months career. I never saw most of the results of
my picture-taking because only a few rolls were sent to
Kodak in Rochester for developing, which was how we
got prints then if we didn't have access to darkrooms,
a feature my school lacked. Not seeing and having the
prints was also not the point. Looking and choosing what
to snap was the point. I am still taking my life, but these
days I see the outcome of what I chose to look at, to print,
to keep or to trash.

The earliest mechanical calculator was called a "difference engine," according to an article I read last night in
The Economist. I woke today thinking that I have a difference engine in my workroom: my dictionary. I use
it to differentiate this from that, correct from mistaken,
here from there, and many more complex distinctions,
including variants of words, all of it counting for clarity
and understanding between people, nations, on a page, a
screen, wherever words are used.

My engine is *The Random House Dictionary of the English Language*, published in 1987, unabridged, at least
according to its title page. I keep that taped-up broken-
backed dog-eared companionable volume close at hand.
I like its generosity of synonyms and antonyms, its distinctions of meaning and spelling, its sample sentences of
usage, its brief derivations of words, and its helpful back
matter that has world maps and flags, small but sufficient
dictionaries of four foreign languages, a basic manual of

grammar and style, proofreader's marks, and many other instructive pages.

The RHD is not as comprehensive as the vast OED, but it does the job for me, waiting patiently for me to touch down on its pages, a landing I control, not some coded process beyond my actual grasp. My dictionary's tangible presence counts in my arithmetic of material things.

Apart from its physicality, I admire the way my old engine has kept its powerful authority. Its say-so is still weighty, clear, and usable. And I enjoy the hint of lost innocence in its outdated slang words. Battered as it is, worn and torn by time and constant handling, it has an impressive grasp of most things that matter to people and their worlds, past and present, and likely tomorrow.

Yet another No, thanks, we regret that your manuscript does not suit our present needs, came in yesterday's mail. I get many standard rejection slips, most of them garnished with a handwritten note signed by the editor: Please try us soon again. That's a little something. Not enough, but more than a brusque electronic Declined from Submittable. I keep those printed slips as documented proof of my official inclusion in a vast global Salon des Refusés of writers. The artists whose paintings were rejected by the conservative Académie for its annual exhibition in 1863 showed their innovative work in a different location. Writers, traditional or experimental, have few alternative places to appear, apart from virtual outlets: e-zines, blogging, and suchlike. Too will-o'-the wisp for me, too fleeting. I want my words on paper, even though paper molders, becomes fodder for silverfish. That could take time, many years of being there.

The 20th Century Limited was an express passenger train that ran between New York and Chicago from 1902 to 1967. I never traveled on that train, but when it was mentioned in a novel I was reading last night, I stopped and thought: Yes! That's it, that's me, a 20th century limited, uncomfortable with the 21st century's light-ning-speed means of communication, tossing restlessly in its flimsy sleeper berth of a fancifully designated cloud, irritated by its instant all-knowingness, troubled by its myopic baggage of selfies, already shunted to a siding, rusting out slowly, eventually to be broken up for scrap iron.

I frequently catch myself wondering about writing while I am doing it. When that happens, I sidetrack to thinking about its uncertainties and assumptions, the satisfaction of arranging words that pin meaning to a page like a specimen fern or a tiger moth, its solitari-ness, the sound and lame hunches, how it stops short without warning, jolting me to a standstill, temporarily anyhow, the whole mixed bag of it that I acknowledge and accept on a more-or-less regular morning schedule.

An aspect of the work l have done for the past fif-teen years continues to mystify me. For a lifelong and resolutely private person, it surprises and rattles me that I changed gears from novels and short stories to personal essays, overriding a habitual reluctance to reveal myself and my shortcomings: overcautiousness, shyness, impatience, a tenuous sense of unworthiness, and some other drawbacks. Did writing become a treatment for what ails me? A shaky foothold on generality? On sociability? A barge to carry my freight away? A belated attempt at shapeshifting? All of the above? I can't answer these questions, I can't even pose them without shuddering.

I just saw a quote in my overstuffed manila folder of scribbled notes: "All that is solid melts into air . . . " I overheard those words at a party many years ago, and they sounded more written than casually spoken, so I looked them up in an anthology of quotations. It is the start of a longer sentence I didn't transcribe, attributed to Karl Marx. Whenever I spot that phrase in my folder, I say it aloud a few times. Its melancholy tone is a cautionary knell. People are solid until they are airy absences, impalpable memories: personal, familial, ancestral, collective. Thwarting our eventual physical unreality is not possible, but there are many ways to concretely postdate a presence, and the written word is one of them.

That said, I don't write with futurity in mind, but for locating and exploring what is on my mind, or was formerly there, and finding words that clarify and convey it, to myself primarily, to others possibly but not necessarily. Am I merely talking to myself? Are there dense clouds of hot air around me like an incubator warming preemie jaundiced inklings and dubious insights?

Even so, soliloquizing, unread by anyone else, there is no other work I would rather be doing until I and/or my mind melt into airy nothing.

In Piermont yesterday for a Sunday stroll with my husband on the pier that stretches to the middle of the Hudson, I could barely take in the big view because I was envisioning something I saw in that river when I was a young girl.

Every now and then, my parents and we four children piled into our car and drove to Bear Mountain. My parents were fans of hiking, up a modest mountain in particular, an enthusiasm popular in Europe, where they were born, raised, and would have stayed if political events hadn't changed their minds in a hurry. They enjoyed the fresh air, the trails through pine-forested slopes and occasional clearings, the sights achieved on reaching summits, the more challenging descent that was hard on the legs. Bear Mountain was nothing like a minor alp above Villars or Interlaken, but it was there, near Manhattan, not too crowded early on a Sunday.

We crossed the George Washington Bridge and took Route 9W to the Bear Mountain parking lot; the Palisades Parkway was still being constructed, and the now-demolished Tappan Zee Bridge was not yet a gleam in a Governor's eye. The Bear

Mountain Bridge was not an option, my mother insisted it was "too narrow and delicate" to be safe. She didn't drive, but she directed.

At several points, 9W ran and still runs near the Hudson River, which gave me a glimpse of something that mattered far more to me than exercise, invigorating air, the perfume of pine trees. It was the sight of rows of gray ships anchored in the Hudson, a mothball fleet, according to my father. Ghost ships was my idea of them. At the speed we drove past that open view to the river, I couldn't see people on their decks, though I now know that every one of those ships was manned with a skeleton crew, which jibes with my view of them as ghostly. Those big gray silent ships were bobbing on currents of a river I knew firsthand, waiting for a war like the one I kept hearing about, a huge fleet of powerful scary ghost destroyers, gunboats, battleships, minelayers, warships that killed people and turned them into ghosts.

I never asked my father to pull over so I could get a better look at those ships, and I never said anything about my idea of them. It was my private business, the business of the oldest child, the only one born in Europe. I didn't have many secrets then, but this was a big one, important, my own, and I kept it to myself long after my childhood when those Bear Mountain excursions took place. Why I wanted to be haunted by the idea of ghost ships and people is a question I haven't yet answered to my own satisfaction. I will keep trying.

The mothball fleet in the Hudson was eventually scrapped. At this moment, there are fleets of warships with skeleton crews anchored in our nation's waters and throughout the world, all waiting for battle duty. Ghosts are still a part of my business, no longer private.

In a burst of clean-up, clear-out activity yesterday, I finally junked the Singer sewing machine my mother gave me many years ago; it had been idle since the long-gone days when she made skirts for her young daughters. I remember seeing paper patterns laid out on the dining room table, but I don't recall watching her use the machine. When I wanted to make cotton bedspreads for my children's rooms, she gladly parted with her old Singer.

I didn't know how to use that machine: There weren't instructions in its case, online help was not yet invented, and my mother away on vacation when I found time for my sewing project. I could, I should manage it on my own, I assured myself. The fabric was cut to the length I needed, the seams would be straight. How hard could it be?

Getting the Singer to work was a lesson in confusion: bobbins here, wheels there, little hooks and spindles everywhere, a pedal below, a needle's eye so narrow I had trouble finding it, and the mysterious appearance of a thread creeping up from under the metal plate when I lowered the threaded needle. I lifted the hinged plate and discovered another bobbin. Aha! Two threads needed for one job. When the fabric was clamped in place, I pressed the pedal, and the Singer sprinted ahead on a raucous track of its own, a clatter of swerving stitches that were nothing like the neat hems I intended to sew. I stopped midway to mayhem, balled up the ruined fabric with its crooked paths of tight stitches, and threw it away. I unplugged the machine, put it in its case, and laid it to rest on the floor of a storage closet. I never attempted to use it again. Buttons apart, I was through with sewing. Except that I wasn't.

The longer I continue to write, a job I began several months after my fiasco with the Singer, the more I see similarities of sewing and writing. There is material: real or invented people, events, places, and numerous words. There are patterns: of grammar, genre, time-tested or innovative. There is stitchery: row after row of sentences threaded together by intention. There is sound: a voice, shrill or soft, a babble, some thunder, occasional music. There is fit: It works or it doesn't. There are needles of criticism, self-generated mostly, mysteries that surface, intents that stray, a mind's wheels turning, narrative and vocabular finishes and flourishes similar to ruffles, embroidery, ornamental braid, frog fastenings.

Notional commonalities are one thing, and facts are another matter. It is a fact that my first computer, a so-called luggable, looked, when closed, almost identical in shape and size to the encased portable Singer, and weighed about the same when carried. I have now discarded both of those machines. I continue to sew buttons and words.

Last night I dreamed I was in an iron lung. I never had polio, though I am old enough to have gotten it in the

years before the Salk vaccine was introduced. My dream
might have been prompted by a television documentary
I saw last week about FDR, in which he is shown frolick-
ing with kids in the pool at Warm Springs, in Georgia, all
of them there for rehabilitative help. FDR couldn't walk
without human or mechanical assistance, but he could
keep his head above water with the support of a life belt
or buoy board, having fun in the pool, laughing and smiling so widely his grin redefines "elasticity."

Why I saw myself in an iron lung puzzles me. Is this
a dream about a coffin? Treading less and less water?
Random bouts of paralysis when facing empty mechanical pages? Playfulness even in the iron jaws of adversity?
Or is it my same old story about the looming harm I
didn't suffer?

On the evening news last night, the newscaster quoted
Joseph Welch's question to Senator Joseph McCarthy,
"Have you no sense of decency, sir, at long last? Have you
left no sense of decency?" This was after reporting on
the current and sensational trial of an elected politician
who for many years systematically looted his district's
school and elder-care funds to buy such luxuries as a
Maserati for a recently purchased mansion with a four-
car garage.

Reminded of the powerful and destructive House Un-
American Activities Committee, it struck me, for the
first time, that my childhood home contained a benign
sort of HUAC, one without self-promoting politicians and

crooked lawyers, the intrigue, the Red Scare, the false accusations, the harmful intentions and results. In our HUAC, my parents were the right-minded committee of two, their agenda, mission was more like it, included creating a version of their past in their new home. Many children of refugees and immigrants newly arrived in America feel they are being raised partly in a parental elsewhere. Language factors in those foreign elsewheres, as does food, traditional customs, manners, holiday rites, education, ambitions, and more. My family's transported locality was Western Europe, their languages French, German and, occasionally, Dutch, the food on our table heavy, their rules, expectations, and hopes for children heavier. I won't speak for my siblings, but I believe they wouldn't quibble with my view of our parental home as a simultaneously real and make-believe place.

Did growing up in a bipartite milieu eventually steer me to the real and make-believe occupational seesaw of writing? I don't have an answer to that question. What I have are feelings, ideas, some memories to unravel, express, and reveal, and that's the hook, line, and sinker of it.

In the stacks at the library last week I saw a copy of *Self-Consciousness*, John Updike's memoir in essays, and it has been on my mind since I glimpsed it. I read it when it was published many years ago. I recall that he wrote about the decades-long wars he waged with his chronically psoriatic skin and his stuttering. My battles aren't visible or audible, much less curable.

I wonder now, this instant, if my long-past reading of Updike's book might have surreptitiously conditioned me to someday relieve my memory's itchy skin by scratching words on it.

Hearing a friend talk about the so-called deep state yesterday cued the thought of a summer I spent in London in my teens with my widowed maternal aunt and her youngest daughter, three months older than I. Our mothers conspired to make us good friends, as they were since girlhood, and simultaneously to spruce up my awkward American ways. Their plot fizzled at the time, my cousin and I weren't close until many years later, but a few steps away from my aunt's house on Thurloe Street, in a café we often went to for the thrill of potential danger and turmoil, plots were as thick as the cream in the buns we ate there. Or so we believed. We had overheard a mention of that café being the seat of the Polish government-in-exile: a shadow cabinet. We didn't know what a shadow government was or how it worked, and we certainly did not want an explanation, the mystery of it was important, scary, intriguing, exotic, even tragic. We couldn't see any of those qualities in the café and its regulars, but we did hear people speaking foreign languages. We could identify French, German, Italian, and Spanish, the thicker harsher sounds we took for Polish, maybe Czech or Hungarian or, alarmingly, Russian. This was in the Cold War Era, Russia was the enemy, powerful and oppressive, much of eastern Europe was subject to Soviet rule. Why we enjoyed being fearful and uninformed is as mysterious as a shadow government was to us at the time. Adolescence doesn't explain it.

Several decades passed before I recognized my own shadow government, and identified it in an essay: its origins, workings, permanence. My cousin is dead, I am steps from over the hill, that café is still there, more of a restaurant now, according to online posts, and I wonder if its shadows haunt the place, darken its ambiance, weigh on the minds of its clients as it failed to do on mine when we sat there seeking mysteries, secrets, adventure, conspiracies, thrills instead of truths.

If wishes were fishes, I would swim on a page, glide, shimmer, coast on currents, turn on a dime, avoid baited hooks of regret and caution, dive to the bottom for solid substance, dazzle with clarity, ease, affection, and candor, leap out of a rushing river for the fun of it, as I am doing here, now, up, for today.

In my cranial cabinet of curiosities there is a collection of words, phrases, images, and ideas, inklings mostly, waiting for me to look at them, handle them, or at least buff them shiny like silver that needs an occasional polish, then reshelve them where they wait for usage, or not. Sometimes they hide in nooks and crannies of their own, and I am "it" in a game I don't enjoy playing but must once in a while. And every once in a longer while, one of those collectibles takes matters into its own hands, so to speak. The word *provenance* flared insistently this morning as I woke, signaling its availability and usefulness.

Questions of provenance are important in the sale of artworks in galleries, even more so in auction houses that handle notably expensive art for resale, with the results reported internationally as big news. Experts examine the authenticity of a work's signature, the identifiable qualities and quirks of its so-called hand, the characteristic subject matter of the artist, and essentially these days, the legitimacy of the owner's, or previous owners', or a museum's claim to the work up for sale.

The question of a claim I make is cloudier, not technical or apparent, not a matter of style or rightful ownership or value or sales-potential. It is experiential, but not something I did or saw or heard. I claim it anyhow, regardless of legitimacy on my part.

When I was a child, an adolescent, a college girl, a young mother, a novice writer of fiction, I worried about being faulted for appropriating an experience I didn't have, not in the flesh. I had it, still do, in the head, where even borrowed pain resides, sleeping and waking on a schedule of its own, or is roused by the owner of the head where it lives. The older I get, the more often I wake that second-hand hurt, and the less I worry about my right to do so. To be sure, many books have now been written about the lasting damage of atrocities and injustices of various sorts and impacts, ongoing anguish felt by generations after the injurious facts, howls and moans of pain that reverberate through the years, forever perhaps. So my head is not unusual in housing the wounds of a war I didn't endure directly. Besides, it contains many more things that are timely, pleasant, ordinary, amusing, dubious, compelling, distracting, and otherwise engaging, all of them waiting for a glance, some attention, a chance.

Acknowledgments

I want to thank everyone who worked with me to make this book a reality. The Bold Story Press team did a stunning and rapid job in bringing the book out. Emily Barrosse, Karen Gulliver, Julianna Scott Fein, Karen Polaski, and everyone else in that office: my admiration and gratitude. Thanks to Meg Wolitzer, Kate Johnson, and Margot Schupf.

The constant and loving support of the entire Bloch family, three generations of it, was crucial, but I want to signal the extraordinary encouragement I got from my husband, Claude, my son, Philippe, and my daughters, Claire and Justine, whose prompt and affectionate attention to whatever help I asked for was near-miraculous. My grandchildren provided expert tech assistance as needed, which is to say: frequently.

My thanks to Jackson Lears, Willard Spiegelman, and Megan Sexton, editors of literary magazines that printed my essays. Their enthusiasm about my work was encouragement that led to this book.

About the Author

Lucienne S. Bloch was born in Belgium, raised in New York City, and graduated from Wellesley College, where she received an Academy of American Poets Award and a prize from the New England Poetry Society. She subsequently worked at New Directions, and then at Random House. After marrying and raising three children, she began writing fiction. Her first novel, *On the Great-Circle Route*, was published by Simon & Schuster. Her second novel, *Finders Keepers*, was published by Houghton Mifflin. One of her short stories was chosen for the PEN Syndicated Fiction Project and is anthologized in *The Sound of Fiction*.

She wrote "Hers" columns for *The New York Times*, was a Resident Fellow at Yaddo, and was awarded a Fellowship in Fiction by the New York Foundation for the Arts. She began writing personal essays sixteen years ago. They have been published in *Raritan*, *North American Review*, *Sewanee Review*, *Southwest Review*, and *Five Points*, and one was excerpted in *Harper's*. Four were cited as Notable in *The Best American Essays* of 2011, 2014, 2017, and 2021.

She lives in New York City with her husband.

CPSIA information can be obtained
at www.ICGtesting.com
Printed in the USA
BVHW030057170323
660607BV00004B/10

9 781954 805446